As one of the world's longest established
and best-known travel brands,
Thomas Cook are the experts in travel.

For more than 135 years our
guidebooks have unlocked the secrets
of destinations around the world,
sharing with travellers a wealth of
experience and a passion for travel.

**Rely on Thomas Cook as your
travelling companion on your next trip
and benefit from our unique heritage.**

Thomas Cook **pocket** guides

HELSINKI

Barbara Radcliffe Rogers
& Stillman Rogers

Your travelling companion since 1873

Thomas
Cook

Written by Barbara Radcliffe Rogers & Stillman Rogers, updated by Jon Sparks

Published by Thomas Cook Publishing
A division of Thomas Cook Tour Operations Limited
Company registration no. 3772199 England
The Thomas Cook Business Park, 9 Coningsby Road,
Peterborough PE3 8SB, United Kingdom
Email: books@thomascook.com, Tel: +44 (0) 1733 416477
www.thomascookpublishing.com

Produced by Cambridge Publishing Management Limited
Burr Elm Court, Main Street, Caldecote CB23 7NU
www.cambridgepm.co.uk

ISBN: 978-1-84848-538-9

© 2006, 2008, 2010 Thomas Cook Publishing
This fourth edition © 2012
Text © Thomas Cook Publishing
Maps © Thomas Cook Publishing/PCGraphics (UK) Limited
Transport map © Communicarta Limited

Series Editor: Karen Beaulah
Production/DTP: Steven Collins

Printed and bound in Spain by GraphyCems

Cover photography © Holger W./Shutterstock

CONTENTS

SYMBOLS KEY

The following symbols are used throughout this book:

ⓐ address ❶ telephone ⓦ website address ⓔ email
🕐 opening times Ⓝ public transport connections ❶ important

The following symbols are used on the maps:

𝒊	information office	▨	point of interest
✈	airport	○	city
➕	hospital	○	large town
🛡	police station	○	small town
🚌	bus station	═	motorway
▤	railway station	—	main road
Ⓜ	metro stop		minor road
✝	cathedral	—	railway
🏙	port		
❶	numbers denote featured cafés & restaurants		

Hotels and restaurants are graded by approximate price as follows:
£ budget price **££** mid-range price **£££** expensive

▶ *Rooftop view towards the Lutheran Cathedral*

INTRODUCING
Helsinki

Introduction

Helsinki's beauty hits you right between the eyes, not least because some of the greatest architects in the world designed its buildings, which are set amid parks and against watery backdrops. Its beauty deserves a closer look, whether it's into shop windows filled with smart Finnish design or inside buildings whose interiors match their stunning façades. But Helsinki is much more than just another pretty face. It is a friendly, exciting, warm-hearted place filled with people whose wry attitude to life will make you laugh, and a nightlife that will keep you dancing into the early hours of the morning. It is blessed by almost round-the-clock sunlight in the summer, when no one ever seems to sleep, and a population that knows how to make the most of the long snowy winter. Join them on skis or snowshoes in the parks, on paths that glitter with lights reflecting in the snow, or skate across the frozen bay of Töölönlahti. Warming up is no problem: take a sauna (you can choose from traditional wood-fired or modern state-of-the-art spas), knock back a steaming cup of *glögi* (mulled wine), go to a jazz club to hear authentic Dixieland, or dance to whatever moves your shoes.

Helsinki seems to be always on the move, with a star-studded line-up of festivals celebrating everything from samba and world cultures to heavy metal and gay pride. Downtown streets rock at night, and the buzz comes from people having a good time, not trying to impress one another with dress or oh-so-cool attitudes. Maybe that's because they know – and know the world knows it, too – that they have a great deal to declare at the customs of fashionable good taste. Whatever's new, you'll see it here first, not because the Finns have rushed out to buy it, but because they have designed it themselves. Here, you'll sense that you are on the cutting edge, whether you're dining on the latest plates from Arabia, drinking out of the newest Iittala stemware, lounging in an Alvar Aalto chair or geeking out on your smartphone.

It's hard not to have a good time in Helsinki, especially when things heat up at night. Perhaps that's the city's biggest surprise – and it's certainly what makes it so much fun to visit.

⬤ *World-famous Finnish design*

When to go

SEASONS & CLIMATE

With northern perversity, Helsinki's climate brings the most rain during the warm summer months, and the best chance of sparkling sunny days in winter. Summer temperatures hover around 20°C (68°F) and winter averages around -4°C (25°F). Winters can be bitterly cold, with temperatures dropping as low as -20°C (-4°F). The most popular months to visit are between May and September, but the city is pleasant year-round, as long as you remember a raincoat in the summer and a warm coat (and boots) in the winter.

Snow is frequent in winter, but rarely deep in the city centre, often melting away quickly. In the rural areas there is permanent snow for the whole winter and it can get deep, especially in northern Finland. Light reflecting off the snow makes the city lighter during the short mid-winter days from November to January, when the sun doesn't rise until late morning and sets by around three in the afternoon.

● *Heavy snowfalls in the park don't deter Helsinki walkers*

ANNUAL EVENTS

January

Art Meets Ice (International Ice Sculpture Competition) Competitors from around the world gather at Korkeasaari Zoo (see page 109) to carve ice into artistic forms, which are left on display until they melt. Advance booking is recommended (tickets: Ⓦ www.lippupalvelu.fi). Ⓦ www.korkeasaari.fi/artmeetsice

DocPoint This documentary festival at the end of January features films not only from Finland and the Baltic states but also from around the world. It celebrates its tenth anniversary in 2012. ⓐ Fredrikinkatu 23 ⓣ 09 672 472 Ⓦ www.docpoint.info

March

Kirkko Soikoon (Church Music Festival) Churches honour Finnish and other Nordic religious music genres by staging orchestral, choral and solo performances in beautiful, contemplative surroundings (tickets: Ⓦ www.lippu.fi or on the door). ⓣ 09 2340 2524 Ⓦ www.kirkkosoikoon.fi

Musica Nova Helsinki Important new music can be heard at this showcase for Finnish and international contemporary composers. The festival is generally held every other year on odd-numbered years. ⓐ Lasipalatsi, Mannerheimintie 22–24 ⓣ 09 6126 5100 Ⓦ www.musicanova.fi

April

April Jazz/Big Band Jazz Festival Finnish and international performers do their best to avoid the melody in concert halls, restaurants and other relaxed (and even ad hoc) venues in Helsinki's neighbouring city (and Finland's second-largest), Espoo. ⓐ Ahertajantie 6 B, Espoo ⓣ 09 455 0003 Ⓦ www.apriljazz.fi

Vappu (30 April) This is Walpurgis Night, cue for one of the biggest parties in Finland, when students gather around Havis Amanda, the mermaid symbol of Helsinki, to drink champagne.

May
Vappupäivä (1 May) The Ullanlinna and Kaisaniemi quarters are the main sites for the lively May Day celebrations, with lots of family-oriented fun, including carnivals.
Evening markets From mid-May, head to the harbour when dusk falls to discover a host of beautifully presented stalls offering foods, handicrafts and other goods.

June
Helsinki Day (12 June) One of the few European capitals that knows its exact birthday, Helsinki marks the occasion with free concerts at Kaivopuisto Park, plus children's events, sports, tours and a market (see page 47). Ⓦ www.helsinkiviikko.fi
Midsummer Eve Finns celebrate at country homes with huge bonfires, *juhannussalko* poles decorated with ribbons and flowers, and many hours of traditional folk music and dance. For those left in the city, there is a celebration at Seurasaari. Tickets are sold at the Tomtebo Folklore Centre (just before the bridge to Seurasaari) or at the office on the island itself. ❶ 09 4050 9660 Ⓦ www.seurasaarisaatio.fi

July
Jazz Espa Free daily jazz performances on Esplanadi and a concert in Alppipuisto. ❶ 09 757 2077 Ⓦ www.jazzliitto.fi
Tuska Open Air Metal Festival Major bands from across Europe and the UK play in Suvilahti. Ⓦ www.tuska-festival.fi

◯ Seurasaari is the venue for Helsinki's main Midsummer celebration

August

Art Goes Kapakka (mid-August) Ten days of music and entertainment right across the city, totalling 250 performances and events in clubs, bars, restaurants, theatres and streets. Ⓦ www.artgoeskapakka.fi

Flow Festival A long weekend of music from all over the world combines music genres from jazz to rock and electronic (tickets: Ⓣ 0600 1 1616 Ⓦ www.tiketti.fi). Ⓐ Vilhonvuorenkatu 11 Ⓣ 09 7931 560 Ⓦ www.flowfestival.com

Helsinki City Marathon The Nordic countries' biggest marathon begins at the Paavo Nurmi statue and winds along the shore and hillsides. Ⓐ Radiokatu 20 Ⓣ 09 3481 2405 Ⓦ www.helsinkicity marathon.com

Helsinki Festival (late August–early September) Featuring prominent international artists in various venues and a festival tent (tickets: Ⓦ www.lippu.fi). The Night of the Arts brings a wide range of street music and art. Ⓣ 09 6126 5100 Ⓦ www.helsinkifestival.fi

September

Design Week Fashion shows, exhibitions and other events, plus a sale of the latest fashions and designer items – the year's best opportunity for a real bargain! Ⓐ Various venues; sale at Kaapelitehdas Ⓣ 09 628 082 Ⓦ www.helsinkidesignweek.com

Helsinki International Film Festival Finland's largest film festival draws upwards of 14,000 people to see flicks of all types from all over the world. Ⓐ Mannerheimintie 22–24 Ⓣ 09 6843 5230 Ⓦ www.hiff.fi

October

Baltic Herring Fair (early October) Fishermen gather in Kauppatori (Market Square) to sell traditional herring products.

A great opportunity to sample local foods as well as boost your Omega 3 intake.

December
Independence Day (6 December) This date kicks off the holiday season, and is also an occasion for processions, visits to cemeteries and gatherings in churches and public places for concerts (which always include Sibelius's *Finlandia*).
St Thomas Christmas Market The finest crafts, foods and arts line Esplanadi, set out in colourful tents to engage the interest of the passer-by (see page 76).
Turku Christmas Market Held in the Old Great Square, with crafts and foods.
Women's Christmas Fair An astonishing variety of fine crafts, all created by Finnish women, fill a market hall at the Wanha Satama (see page 77).

PUBLIC HOLIDAYS
New Year's Day 1 Jan
Epiphany 6 Jan
Easter 6–9 Apr 2012, 29 Mar–1 Apr 2013, 18–21 Apr 2014
May Day 1 May
Ascension Day 17 May 2012, 9 May 2013, 29 May 2014
Midsummer Eve & Midsummer Day 22 & 23 June 2012, 21 & 22 June 2013, 20 & 21 June 2014
All Saints 3 Nov 2012, 2 Nov 2013, 1 Nov 2014
Independence Day 6 Dec
Christmas 24–6 Dec

The National Romantics

Finland's version of Romantic Nationalism was similar to other countries' in that it sprang from a desire for independence. By the turn of the 20th century, the people we know as the Finns were reacting against years of control, first by the Swedes, and then by Russia. Their wish for an identity and cultural heritage of their own focused primarily on the *Kalevala*, a national saga that was a compendium of folk tales from the rural heartland of Karelia. These stories' motifs and themes, which are evident in Finnish culture today, were met by an influx of new ideas that came from the European Arts and Crafts movement and the *Jugendstil* aesthetic; this synthesis of ancient and modern cultural phenomena resulted in the emergence of a group of brilliant young artists, including Jean Sibelius (whose *Finlandia* is a pure expression of national pride) and the painters Akseli Gallen-Kallela and Helene Schjerfbeck.

Pre-eminent among these virtuosos were the architects Herman Gesellius, Armas Lindgren and Eliel Saarinen, who met at Helsinki's Polytechnic Institute, formed a consultancy, and soon began to wield an immense influence on the local, national and international stages. The trio developed *Jugendstil* (German for 'youth style') architecture into a style called National Romantic, a form that was directly influenced by the Karelian architectural heritage. They designed some of Helsinki's most prominent buildings, such as the Ateneum and Helsinki Railway Station (see pages 71 & 66). Finnish National Romanticism really came to the world's attention at the Paris World Exposition of 1900 (at which time Finland was still a grand duchy of the Russian Empire), thanks to the sensation caused by the drama, dynamism and dash of Saarinen's pavilion. In fact, Paris 1900 almost certainly marks the birth of what the world would come to admire as Finnish design, which, despite the fact that the Finns' independence has removed the catalyst of artistic urgency, has prospered and evolved, and, some might allege, reached its zenith thus far with the Nokia E7 smartphone. Or was it the Oma lemon squeezer?

The National Museum of Finland exemplifies the National Romantic Style

History

At a latitude of 60° north, Helsinki is the northernmost of all continental European capitals, with a prime location on the Baltic. Its historical position as the bridge between Russia and the West made Finland a pawn between the rulers of Sweden – once a great European power – and Russia. During Swedish rule the provincial capital was at Turku; it was Swedish King Gustav Vasa who established a trading port at Helsinki in 1550.

This busy port settlement gradually grew in importance, until the early 1700s dealt it a double blow: in 1710 the plague nearly wiped out its 2,000 inhabitants; then, in 1713, the Swedes burned it down to keep it from falling into the hands of Peter the Great. To protect the harbour from future attacks, Sweden built the great Suomenlinna Fortress (see page 110). However, Russian harassment continued to slow the city's growth.

A century after the plague, two more events changed Helsinki irrevocably. A fire in 1808 devastated most of the city and, before it was rebuilt, the province was ceded to Russia in 1809, ending Swedish rule. Finland became the semi-autonomous Russian Grand Duchy of Finland, and Tsar Alexander I lavished attention on his new city on the Baltic. He brought in the German-born architect Carl Ludvig Engel, who had designed much of St Petersburg. Engel remodelled Helsinki, especially around Senate Square, and gave it the elegance that it retains today. In 1812 Alexander I moved the capital of the Grand Duchy from Turku to Helsinki, and the city has been the capital ever since.

Rapid industrialisation from the 1860s to the beginning of the 20th century meant equally rapid population growth, and with it came the need for new neighbourhoods. Building after building sprang out of this boom, especially at the turn of the century, when Helsinki acquired a remarkable number of *Jugendstil* structures by such luminaries as Eliel Saarinen, Armas Lindgren and their contemporaries. At the same time, a growing feeling of nationalism pushed the country toward independence.

Finland seized the moment when revolution rocked Russia in 1917: Parliament declared independence on 6 December and, after a short civil war, a republic was declared in 1919, with Helsinki as its capital. Since then, with the exception of the period of war with the Soviet Union in the 1940s, Helsinki has grown as an industrial and innovatory centre at the forefront of the Nordic design phenomenon. Since the 1952 Olympics it has also been a centre for major sporting events, and a prime location for the development of international diplomatic initiatives. Finland became a member of the European Union since 1995. The country's first female president, Tarja Halonen, has been in power since 2001. The next presidential election will be held in January 2012.

◉ *The ordeal of World War II is commemorated at Hietaniemi Cemetery*

Lifestyle

It was the Finns who invented the sauna, despite occasional claims to the contrary from Sweden. For most Finns, the chance to relax in extreme heat is one of life's civilising rituals, and they're likely to fit one in at any time of day, as the urge takes them. Saunas are the venues for business meetings, family gatherings and all kinds of social interplay, which explains why they're found all over the

⬤ *Out and about in the occasional snowstorm*

city, sometimes in the unlikeliest of locations. Proximity to a lake is a definite bonus, since the Finns are great believers in a quick plunge into cold water after – or during – a sauna.

Though often believed to be taciturn, the Finns can actually be quite voluble in social situations, especially when loosened up with a little alcohol. They also have a wicked sense of humour, which is often very dry and sly, along with a keen sense of the ridiculous. They can laugh at themselves, and their apparent self-deprecation is a popular national joke with them. It is also true, however, that a group of Finns can sit in a room together quite happily without uttering a word, and be quite comfortable. So don't be alarmed if silence appears to descend the very minute you enter almost any social setting. And expect silence in the sauna, unless you're in a business meeting. Saunas, incidentally, are always gender-divided, except for those owned or popularly used by families. The same applies at the nude beach at Seurasaari, which has separate sections for men and women. A second nude 'beach' (actually a rather rocky bit of shoreline) on Pihlajasaari is, however, unisex.

Finns are generally easy-going and have a live-and-let-live attitude, so although Helsinki doesn't have the gay scene of, say, Stockholm, gay travellers are welcome and excite little attention. There are several gay clubs in the city, but most of them welcome heterosexuals, too. When it comes to clothes, Finns are usually casual, though they like to put their glad rags on for a big night out. They dress for the climate, so it's not unusual to see boots and thick ski jackets in the cloakrooms of upmarket restaurants in the winter. The Finns are pretty sensible people, who don't get huffy over dress codes or have bouncers to protect self-consciously cool venues from the criminally under-preened. The Finns go out to have a good time, and they are happy for you to have a good time, too.

Culture

The fact that Finland has such a distinct culture of its own is remarkable, considering that this small country spent so much of its past being tossed back and forth between two other – and very strong – cultures. That the Finnish language has remained distinct and in steady use is equally surprising. Today, just enough of the Russian and Swedish flavours remain in Finnish culture to make for an interesting balance.

What does predominate is the Finnish sense of style. Leaders in modern design, the Finns are the epitome of the Nordic aesthetic – clean lines, fresh concepts and functional designs that look sharp and work well. Whether it's a building, a mobile phone, sportswear or a kitchen appliance, if it's designed in Finland, it will combine the often-conflicting needs of form and function into one graceful whole. Interest in design is more than a trade commodity, it's a national passion, because the Finns genuinely revel in being surrounded by well-designed things, whether they are the world's most comfortable scissors (Fiskars) or stylish home accessories (Marimekko® or Arabia). This has been recognised with the designation of Helsinki as World Design Capital 2012.

Design District Helsinki (see page 62) is the place to revel in this Finnish phenomenon. In the space of a few streets, you'll find the Design Museum (see page 71), the Museum of Finnish Architecture (see page 76) and the Design Forum shop (see page 79), as well as galleries and designer boutiques.

Other arts hold a high place in Finnish culture, too. Foreigners may be surprised to see enthusiastic fans of all ages in audiences at the opera or classical music concerts. Finns are likely to have the works of Finnish artists hanging on their walls. Finland's architects

🔺 *Marimekko® is one of the most famous Finnish design brands*

A RACE APART

Although Finland is most definitely a Nordic country, and culturally has gained a lot from its long connection with Sweden, the Finns are not primarily of the same northern Germanic stock as their neighbours on the Scandinavian Peninsula, and their language is also distinct. No one knows for sure how long the Finns have been living in the Baltic or exactly where their ancestors came from, but the Finnish language belongs to a group that includes Estonian and Hungarian, and is entirely unrelated to the Indo-European languages that nearly all of the rest of Europe speaks.

are world famous, and the Finns value their creativity just as much as the rest of the world, so you'll see examples of their work at every turn. Helsinki residents are far more likely to know the name of a local building's architect than are residents of any other city in Europe.

Helsinki is filled with performance venues for everything from opera and dance to rock concerts and sports competitions. Tickets are refreshingly well priced – those for the Philharmonic Orchestra concerts cost between €6 and €25, for example. For tickets to various concert and theatre venues, contact **Lippupalvelu** (🕿 0600 1 08 00 🌐 www.lippupalvelu.fi), **Tiketti** (🕿 0600 1 16 16 🌐 www.tiketti.fi) or **Lippu** (🕿 0600 900 900 🌐 www.lippu.fi). For other listings media, see page 32.

● *Tourists admiring the view from the steps of the Lutheran Cathedral*

 # MAKING THE MOST OF
Helsinki

Shopping

The streets bordering Esplanadi and the parallel Aleksanterinkatu lead to Mannerheimintie, forming the centre of Helsinki's most fashionable (and pricey) shopping district. To the south and west lies the Design District Helsinki (see page 62) where you'll find designer shops selling everything from paper clips to coffee pots, and Fredrikinkatu, lined with boutiques and music shops. In the market at the harbour (see page 68), you'll find fresh local farm products, crafts and Russian fur hats, with more foods sold in the striped market hall. At the western edge of the city is the restored Hietalahti Market Hall and a giant flea market (see page 97) across the square from the historic Market Hall, where you can get anything from last year's clothing to family heirlooms – all at rock-bottom prices.

Shops are generally open from 09.00 or 10.00 to 18.00 or 20.00 Monday to Friday and 09.00 to 14.00 Saturday. Most shops close on Sundays, though major department stores often open on Sundays from June to August and before Christmas.

Distinctive Finnish products to look for are glassware (big names are Iittala, Nuutajärvi and Arabia), fur and leather clothing, traditional and contemporary jumpers and jerseys, and beautiful wooden utensils and furnishings. Exquisite kitchenware, carved in graceful and flowing forms out of velvet-smooth local woods, includes spoons, spatulas and cake servers. Foods you may want to take back with you after you've tasted them are cloudberry or lingonberry preserve, smoked reindeer or salmon, and the incomparable Finnish honey.

Local crafts, found in handwork and museum shops and in markets, vary widely. Rustic reindeer made of bundled straw, or hand-knitted traditional woollen hats, socks and mittens are sold alongside the sleek, modern designs for which the Nordic countries are so well known. In Helsinki's shops you'll find Sámi crafts from Lapland, such as reindeer-bone jewellery and carved birchwood cups. Look for the *duodji* label, guaranteeing that these are genuine Sámi crafts.

The good news for non-European shoppers is that Finland's 22 per cent VAT is often refundable for those who are not residents of the European Union. The easiest way to avoid receiving separate euro cheques from each shop (these may cost you more than their value to cash) is to use the Global Blue refund service. Ask for a refund cheque at any shop displaying a 'Tax Free' logo. At the airport, have these stamped at the Global Blue refund desk and collect your refund in cash.

USEFUL SHOPPING PHRASES

What time do they open/close?
Milloin se avataan/suljetan?
Mil-loin she ervertahn/suljehtahn?

How much is it?
Paljonko se maksaa?
Perlyonko she merksah?

I'd like to buy ...
Haluaisin ostaa ...
Herlu-aisin ostah ...

Eating & drinking

It's true that Finnish cuisine has not yet rocked the European charts, but several of Helsinki's chefs certainly have. The best of them revel in the ingredients of the surrounding water and land – seafood from the Baltic and Finland's lakes, vegetables and berries whose flavours become concentrated as they ripen in the long hours of summer sun, wild berries from the north, forest mushrooms and game from the tundra and fells. A number of Helsinki's restaurants offer special menus of these local ingredients at the height of their season, as part of an initiative called HelsinkiMenu.

Complicated preparations are shunned in favour of those that let the natural flavours of fresh ingredients shine through. Chefs draw on the traditional influences of Finland, Russia and Sweden, as well as an eclectic mix that ranges from Asian to Mediterranean. While you can find French, Italian, Chinese, Thai and even Irish pub food here, you'll eat best when you seek Finnish chefs working with their own native ingredients.

Meals are normally served in three courses, often beginning with a warming hearty soup in the winter. Pork, lamb and beef are common main-course meats, and many menus offer reindeer in some form. Bear is usually served in Russian restaurants (Helsinki's are known for being better than those in St Petersburg), as a stew or smoked.

PRICE CATEGORIES

Price ratings for restaurants in this book are based on the average cost of a main course for one person.

£ up to €15 ££ €15–25 £££ over €25

🔺 *Finns make the most of the summer by eating outdoors as much as possible*

Baltic herring, *silakka*, is the favourite fish, fried, grilled, baked with layers of potato and cream or pickled as a snack. Herring is also smoked or marinated in a way similar to gravadlax, which is made with salmon. Arctic char, trout, salmon and whitefish are popular, and crayfish are in season during August and September.

In the autumn, markets are piled high with woodland mushrooms (mostly) from Lapland, and chefs take full advantage of this bounteous supply. Chanterelles are the tastiest of these, but you'll see all sorts, in meat dishes or served on their own.

Makkara (sausages) are the snack food of choice, and you'll find them sizzling on grills in markets and on street stalls. They may be made from pork or any other meat, and are always delicious. *Mustamakkara*, from Tampere, is essentially a black pudding, and is usually served with sweet-tart lingonberry jam.

Lingonberries and earthy-sweet cloudberries ripen in the autumn, but you'll find them as jams and condiments and in desserts any time of year. Cloudberries are an especially rare delicacy, but they will be on the menus of better restaurants, frequently as a topping for puddings and ice cream. Pastries and baked goods are excellent, and the Finns enjoy these with their coffee at cafés and bakeries. Sweet coffee breads are popular, as is *karjalanpiirakat*, a savoury pastry from eastern Finland, with a filling of rice. Breads are varied and very good, ranging from dark rye to a snowy-white bread made with potatoes. Crisp flatbreads are usually made of rye flour.

Breads are always part of a full breakfast (a meal that is usually quite hearty), with a hot dish of eggs and meat and often porridge, or a buffet of cold cuts and cheeses – and plenty of coffee, although tea will always be offered, too.

Wine is available at most restaurants, with some having outstanding wine lists. Local alcoholic drinks include vodka, schnapps and liqueurs made from native berries. Look especially for *lakka*, made of cloudberries, and *mesimarja*, made of highly flavoured Arctic brambleberries. *Olut* (beer) is the main drink, not least in the sauna. Major brands like Lapin Kulta and Karhu are decent-standard lagers, but there are many more interesting offerings to be found, with various brewery-restaurants leading the way. In the winter, you'll be offered *glögi*, a tasty blend of red wine, spices, raisins, almonds and blackcurrant juice. There are many recipes for this. At any winter market, you'll find at least one steaming black cauldron of *glögi*.

Breakfast is normally served from 07.00 to 10.00, and lunch begins early, at 11.00. The evening meal is also served early, often from 16.00 or 17.00, but continues late into the evening, with many restaurants serving until 23.00. At midday you may opt for a light lunch or a full meal. The latter is often a bargain, at a set price as low as €8. Advance booking is wise for popular restaurants, especially on Wednesday, Friday and Saturday evenings. If meeting Finnish friends for a meal (or any other occasion), remember that they are prompt and value punctuality. If you are delayed for more than five minutes, phone them – they will be carrying a mobile.

Service charges are usually included in restaurant bills, but a modest tip is always welcome if service has been attentive. Give this directly to the server in cash, rather than adding it to the bill. Smoking is banned in public places.

USEFUL DINING PHRASES

I would like a table for ... people
Saadaanko me pöytä ...
Sahdahnko meh per-ewta ...

May I see the menu?
Voisinko nähdä menun?
Voi-shinko nahkh-da mehnun?

I am a vegetarian
Olen kasvissyöjä
Olehn kers-vis-sewer-ya

May I have the bill?
Saisinko laskun?
Sai-sinko lerksun?

Where is the toilet (restroom)?
Missa on vessa?
Missa on vessah?

Entertainment & nightlife

With almost 10 per cent of its population being university students, Helsinki is among Europe's hippest cities, with non-stop nightlife that's all the better for being largely undiscovered by foreigners. Don't worry about feeling left out, though, since almost everyone under 40 speaks excellent English. Variety is the name of Helsinki's game, with everything from clubs run by film directors to jazz clubs, gay clubs, raucous pubs and heavy-metal karaoke bars.

Without, perhaps, the pretension of Stockholm, but with all its variety and cool, Helsinki's night scene is user-friendly. There are no dress codes here – you'll want to be smartly dressed, but no ties are required and, as we've said, no bouncers will be at the door selecting clientele on the basis of their designer labels. Age is another matter, since clubs set their own rules. If you're over 24, you're home free; between 20 and 24 you may not be allowed into some clubs, especially on busy nights. A few places welcome anyone over 18, especially in the area around the Kamppi metro station, a popular area for under-20s.

The hot nights are Friday and Saturday, but Wednesday is also often busy. Expect to pay about €5 for admission to clubs, more for those with live music, plus another €1–2 for the compulsory coat check. A glass of beer or wine is usually about €5–6 in pubs, more in some clubs.

Nightlife is hottest in the streets around the railway station (unlike in many other cities, this area is prime real estate), along Esplanadi and immediately south, between Mannerheimintie and Fredrikinkatu, west of Mannerheimintie between Finlandia Hall and the National Opera, and in the streets south of Uudenmaankatu, as far as Kapteeninkatu. An up-and-coming area for pubs is Kallio, where the previously grungy atmosphere is becoming increasingly hip.

As with anywhere else in the world, scuffles may break out as night fades into morning. So if the atmosphere begins to take on an angry tone, slip quietly away.

Clubs are not the only place young Finns spend a night out. Live performances are everywhere: arena rock shows, experimental metal, pop and a summer packed with festivals that always include music, often free. Besides the highbrow halls for opera, ballet and classical music (all well attended by people of all ages), venues include the **Savoy Theatre** (ⓐ Kasarminkatu 46 ⓣ 09 3101 2000 ⓦ www.savoyteatteri.fi) for stage performances by Finnish and touring companies that range from classical theatre to contemporary and occasional musical shows; **Olympic Stadium** (see page 88), home to all the big summer concerts; and the somewhat smaller **Hartwall Areena** (ⓐ Areenakuja ⓣ 0204 1997 ⓦ www.hartwall-areena.com), where even headliners such as Eric Clapton, Prince and Plácido Domingo perform. At the smaller **House of Culture** (ⓐ Sturenkatu 4 ⓣ 09 774 0270 ⓦ www.kulttuuritalo.fi) you'll hear metal, rock and pop. Tickets for the latter two venues are available from ⓦ www.lippu.fi or ⓦ www.lippupalvelu.fi (see page 22).

Another good option for a relatively cheap and cheerful night out, particularly if it's raining or you're with children, is the cinema. Cinema programmes are available from hotels and the tourist office. The widest choice is at **Tennispalatsi** (see page 105) with 14 screens, and **Kinopalatsi** (ⓐ Kaisaniemenkatu 2 ⓣ 0600 007 007 ⓦ www.finnkino.fi), with 10. The selection is international and all films are shown in their original language with Finnish subtitles. Soundtracks are very rarely dubbed. **The Orion** (ⓐ Eerikinkatu 15 ⓣ 09 615 400 ⓦ www.kava.fi) is home to the Finnish Film Archive, which shows three films every day except Mondays. Tickets at the major cinemas are about €10 for evening shows (often cheaper earlier in the day); smaller venues cost less. Book ahead for Friday and Saturday evenings.

Before you travel to Helsinki, it's worth finding out what's on during your stay and booking tickets if necessary. Helsinki City Tourist & Convention Bureau (see page 153) has up-to-date information on what's happening at all venues, including clubs. Before you go, visit Ⓦ www.visithelsinki.fi, and click on 'brochures' to download publications filled with the latest news on what's hot in entertainment and clubs. The *Nordic Oddity* brochure, available on this website, contains insider tips.

When you arrive in Helsinki, pick up a copy of the twice-monthly *City-lehti* for listings of current happenings – it is free at most shops and hotels. *Helsinki This Week*, the tourist office's magazine in English, is also free, and available everywhere. It is stronger on restaurant information and has a good calendar of events for the current month, in addition to seasonal features. For a complete listing of the many summer music festivals in Finland, see Ⓦ www.festivals.fi

Tickets for events at most major venues are available through either Lippu, Lippupalvelu or Tiketti (see page 22).

○ Time your visit to coincide with one of Finland's many summer festivals

Sport & relaxation

Don't abandon your fitness routine in Helsinki – this is an exercise-friendly, go-for-it town, with parks and paths everywhere. The Finns are great walkers, runners, skiers, skaters and cyclists, so exercise is a good way to mingle with locals, too.

PARTICIPATION SPORTS

Fishing

All that sparkling clean water surrounding the city will tempt anglers, and all they need is a traveller's fishing permit from Stockmann department store (see page 80) or a fishing shop. The shore around the Old Town Rapids is reserved for fishing. See Ⓦ www.ahven.net for further information.

Jogging & cycling

The most popular jogging routes are around Töölö Bay and the shore at Vanhankaupunginkoski (Old Town Rapids). To enjoy the network of bike paths between sights, borrow a free City Bike (€2 deposit) from any of the green racks.

● *All of Helsinki's large parks have ski trails*

Winter sports

Cross-country skiing is extremely popular, with over 180 km (112 miles) of dedicated trails within the city limits. The **Paloheinä Recreational Centre** (🄰 Pakilantie 124 🄵 09 8775 2281 🄽 Bus: 66, 66A) also offers rental skis, boots and poles. Trails, lit after dark, open as early as November and may have snow into April. Skating rinks are everywhere, but the **Kallion Tekojäärata** (🄰 Helsinginkatu 23 🄵 09 3103 1643 🄻 Mid-Nov–mid-Mar 🄽 Tram: 1A, 3B, 8) and the **Helsinki Icepark** (🄰 Next to train station on Rautatientori 🄵 040 334 5617 🄦 www.icepark.fi 🄻 Late Nov–mid-Mar) have music and rental skates.

RELAXATION

Swimming & saunas

The Olympic-size pools at the outdoor **Swimming Stadium** (🄰 Hammerskjöldintie 5 🄵 09 3108 7854 🄻 May–mid-Sept 🄽 Tram: 3T, 7) and the indoor **Mäkelänrinne Swimming Centre** (🄰 Makelankatu 49 🄵 09 3484 8800 🄦 www.urheiluhallit.fi 🄻 06.15–21.00 Mon–Fri, 08.00–20.00 Sat, 09.00–20.00 Sun 🄽 Tram: 1, 1A, 7) are open to the public, or you can combine swimming with a real cultural fix at Helsinki's oldest traditional swimming hall, the **Yrjönkatu Swimming Hall** (🄰 Yrjonkatu 21 🄵 09 3108 7401), which also has a sauna. Bathing suits are not worn here, so men and women swim at different times; the schedule is available at most hotels. The best beaches are at Seurasaari, Suomenlinna and Pihlajasaari.

Of course, you shouldn't miss the most Finnish of all activities – a sauna. The 70-year-old **Kotiharjun** (🄰 Harjutorinkatu 1 🄵 09 753 1535 🄦 www.kotiharjunsauna.fi) is the city's last old-fashioned wood-burning (as opposed to electric) sauna, which makes for an interesting twist. For more options in Helsinki, visit 🄦 www.sauna.fi. For some real luxury, steal away to the Naantali Spa, near Turku (see page 140).

Accommodation

For a Nordic capital, Helsinki offers some surprisingly moderate hotel rates. Of course, you can luxuriate in grandeur, but there are more budget options here than in many other Nordic cities. Even the finest hotels, such as Hotel Kämp, offer special promotions, especially at weekends. Always ask about these when booking.

Most hotels are centrally located, and nearly all are close to public transportation. Unlike in many cities, you needn't worry about avoiding the area close to the railway station, since this is an excellent neighbourhood in the midst of the best shopping and attractions.

The **Helsinki Expert** booking service (❶ 09 2288 1400 Ⓦ www.helsinkiexpert.fi ❶ 09.00–18.00 Mon–Fri, 10.00–18.00 Sat & Sun (June–Aug); 09.00–18.00 Mon–Fri, 10.00–17.00 Sat (Sept–May)) is located at the railway station and handles hotels, hostels and smaller guest houses. For information on hostels, contact the **Finnish Youth Hostel Association** (Ⓦ www.srm.fi).

HOTELS

Finn £ Just over half a kilometre (a third of a mile) from the railway station, this is a small but comfortable and reasonably priced hotel. All 27 rooms have private facilities, TV and phone, and some have a shower. A pool and saunas are next door. ❸ Kalevankatu 3B (Western & northern Helsinki) ❶ 09 684 4360 Ⓦ www.hotellifinn.fi Ⓜ Metro: Kamppi

Omena Hotel Eerikinkatu £ With an automated check-in system, this is the ultimate in anonymity, but it's also one of the most economical options in Helsinki, and pretty central, too. It is especially

PRICE CATEGORIES
Price ratings for accommodation are based on the average rate
for a double room for one night (usually including breakfast).
£ up to €90 **££** €90–190 **£££** over €190

good value for couples. ❸ Eerikinkatu 24 (Western & northern
Helsinki) ❶ 020 1234 608 ❻ www.omenahotels.com
❼ Metro: Kamppi

Arthur £–££ A handsome and recently refurbished small hotel
within a few hundred metres of the railway station and the best
shopping in the city. Weekend rates for a standard double are under
€100. The on-site restaurant is well regarded. ❸ Vuorikatu 19
(Esplanadi & the harbour) ❶ 09 173 441 ❻ www.hotelarthur.fi
❼ Metro: Kaisaniemi

Crowne Plaza Helsinki ££ The Crowne Plaza is a large, multi-storey,
modern, glass-fronted building at the very heart of city life. The
beautifully appointed modern rooms have everything, including
high-speed Internet connections. The fitness facilities, which
incorporate a large pool, are impressive, too. ❸ Mannerheimintie 50
(Western & northern Helsinki) ❶ 09 2521 1001 ❻ www.crowneplaza-
helsinki.fi ❼ Metro: Rautatientori; tram: 4, 7, 10

Cumulus Kaisaniemi ££ Another business-travel hotel, close to
downtown. Clean, comfortable and friendly. ❸ Kaisaniemenkatu 7
(Esplanadi & the harbour) ❶ 09 172 881 ❻ www.cumulus.fi
❼ Metro: Kaisaniemi

Helka ££ Rooms at this centrally located hotel were recently refurbished with funky décor and furniture; all have private bathrooms, TVs and phones. Further facilities include saunas and a whirlpool for relaxation, and a bar and restaurant. It's a business hotel, so rates are reduced at weekends. ❸ Pohjoinen Rautatiekatu 23 (Western & northern Helsinki) ❶ 09 613 580 Ⓦ www.helka.fi Ⓝ Metro: Kamppi

Sokos Hotel Presidenttii ££ Immaculate, if unsurprising, modern hotel in an excellent central position practically on top of the Kamppi bus/metro station. It has fast free Wi-Fi throughout, a pleasant in-house bar and a guest sauna. ❸ Eteläinen Rautatiekatu 4 (Western & northern Helsinki) ❶ 020 771 6555 Ⓦ www.sokoshotels.fi Ⓝ Metro: Kamppi

Glo ££–£££ This new boutique hotel offers 144 sleekly designed, generously sized rooms with trendy extras such as flat-screen TVs and Wi-Fi. Staff go out of their way to accommodate special requests. Carlito's gourmet pizzeria serves carefully designed pizzas with first-class ingredients. ❸ Kluuvikatu 4 (Esplanadi & the harbour) ❶ 010 344 4400 Ⓦ www.palacekamp.fi Ⓝ Metro: Kaisaniemi

Hotel Katajanokka ££–£££ A truly unique chance to spend a night in jail without having broken the law. This former prison was turned into a luxury hotel in 2007. ❸ Merikasarminkatu 1a (Esplanadi & the harbour) ❶ 09 686 450 Ⓦ www.bwkatajanokka.fi Ⓝ Tram: 4T

Linna ££–£££ A fabulous *Jugendstil* building houses the reception and main facilities of the Linna, while its comfortable rooms are in a

⬥ Glo is one of the city's best hotels

modern extension behind. ⓐ Lönnrotinkatu 29 (Western & northern Helsinki) ⓣ 010 344 4100 ⓦ www.palacekamp.fi ⓝ Tram: 6

Rivoli Jardin ££–£££ Close to Esplanadi and the activities of the central district, this elegant, family-run boutique hotel has 55 rooms, plus a wide range of business features including Internet access. There's also an on-site sauna. Apartments are available and you can even bring your dog. ⓐ Kasarmikatu 40 (Esplanadi & the harbour) ⓣ 09 681 500 ⓦ www.rivoli.fi ⓝ Tram: 9, 10

Scandic Grand Marina ££–£££ This hotel, in a brilliantly converted 1913 warehouse designed by architect Lars Sonck, boasts elegant modern rooms. Excellent location on the harbour, opposite the ferry terminal. ⓐ Katajanokanlaituri 7 (Esplanadi & the harbour) ⓣ 09 16 661 ⓦ www.scandichotels.fi ⓝ Tram: 4

Hotel Kämp £££ Stunningly restored, this grand hotel dating from 1887 has service to match, with facilities such as a day spa and one of the city's best fine dining experiences in Restaurant Kämp Signé. The location, near Esplanadi, is superb, and the breakfast buffet outstanding. ⓐ Pohjoisesplanadi 29 (Esplanadi & the harbour) ⓣ 09 576 111 ⓦ www.hotelkamp.fi ⓝ Tram: 3T, 4, 7

HOSTELS

Eurohostel £ This hostel has 255 beds in 135 rooms; singles, doubles, triples and family rooms are available. The recently repainted rooms have TVs and new furniture, and there are self-catering facilities on each floor. Rates include a morning sauna. Shared bathrooms. ⓐ Linnankatu 9 (Esplanadi at the harbour) ⓣ 09 622 0470 ⓦ www.eurohostel.fi ⓝ Tram: 4

Hostel Suomenlinna £ If the idea of staying in a fortress appeals, this is the place for you. A fascinating sight in itself, the island fortress (see page 110) was built by the Swedes and reinforced by the Russians as a primary defence for the city. The hostel has 40 beds, in rooms for between two and ten people, plus a café and a self-catering kitchen. Showers and toilets are shared. It's only a 15-minute ferry ride from the city centre. ⓐ Suomenlinna C 9 (The islands & outskirts) ⓣ 09 684 7471 ⓦ www.snk.fi/suomenlinna ⓝ Ferry from Kauppatori

Stadion Hostel £ A friendly, comfortable hostel in the Olympic Stadium. There are 167 beds, available in dormitories and private rooms. There's a shared kitchen but breakfast is also offered. ⓐ Pohjoinen Stadiontie 4 (Western & northern Helsinki) ⓣ 09 477 8480 ⓦ www.stadionhostel.com ⓝ Tram: 3T, 7B (get off at Auroran sairaala)

CAMPSITE
Rastila Camping Camping in the city is possible here, a 15–20 minute ride from the railway station. The on-site restaurant is open in summer. ⓐ Karavaanikatu 4 (The islands & outskirts) ⓣ 09 3107 8517 ⓦ www.rastilacamping.fi ⓝ Train: Rastila

THE BEST OF HELSINKI

If you only have a few days to spend in Helsinki, you may be tempted to concentrate on the eastern half of the city centre, but you should try to make time to visit some of the sights of the western and northern areas and definitely take a harbour trip to see this fascinating metropolis from a different angle.

TOP 10 ATTRACTIONS

- **Suomenlinna Fortress** One of the world's largest sea fortresses and a UNESCO World Heritage Site to boot on a cluster of islands commanding the approaches to the harbour (see page 110).

- **Boat trips around the archipelago** Admire the city from all angles on an excursion boat or a ferry trip to the islands (see page 106).

- **Uspenski Cathedral** The Russian presence of western Europe's largest Orthodox church still makes an impression (see page 70).

- **Kauppatori (Market Square) and harbour** The real heart of Helsinki, where locals, visitors, craftspeople and traders all meet (see page 68).

- **Design Museum** The evolution of style periods expressed in numerous materials and objects. Brilliant design, brilliantly displayed (see page 71).

- *Jugendstil* **buildings** Take a walking tour as one of the best ways to see Helsinki's fabulous architecture (see page 64).

- **Seurasaari Open-Air Museum** Historic buildings from all over Finland are here at this island museum with its working farm, which is also the centre for Helsinki's Midsummer celebrations (see page 114).

- **Korkeasaari Zoo** Snow leopards, Siberian tigers, Asian lions: big cat heaven – and plenty more besides (see page 109).

- **Temppeliaukio Church** Also known as Church in the Rock; enjoy its unique atmosphere any time, or savour its great acoustics at an unforgettable concert (see page 91).

- **Finnish design** The latest and coolest – see it first in Design District Helsinki, the area around Diana Park (see page 62).

⬤ *The Pohjola Building: design by Eliel Saarinen, sculptures by Hilda Flodin*

Suggested itineraries

HALF-DAY: HELSINKI IN A HURRY

If you're unlucky enough to have only half a day free, you can still use it to absorb a lot of the sights and sounds of the city. Begin at the market, right on the harbour, for a preview of what you'll see on tonight's menu and to mix with the hearty, good-humoured Finns. Make a detour east to see the interior of Uspenski Cathedral (see page 70) before heading uphill from the market to Senate Square (see page 70). Head west on Aleksanterinkatu, past the smart shops, stepping into No 44, the Pohjola Insurance Building (see page 68), for a dose of Finnish *Jugendstil*. Don't miss the big square, Rautatientori, bordered by the National Theatre (see page 75), the Ateneum (see page 71) and Saarinen's landmark railway station (see page 66). Beyond the station, take a left on Mannerheimintie, then left again to circle back to the harbour along Esplanadi (see page 64). This walk will take you to some more landmark sights, the best of Helsinki's shops and some great cafés (Café Engel on Senate Square or Café Kappeli on Esplanadi (see page 82) are local favourites).

1 DAY: TIME TO SEE A LITTLE MORE

If you have completed the morning's whistle-stop tour and have acquired a feel for the architecture, design and lively buzz of the city, use the afternoon to take a boat to the fortress archipelago of Suomenlinna (see page 110). The 15-minute trip gives good city views, and once you're on the island you can explore the fortress buildings, watch the visitor centre's excellent film, visit the museums and craft studios, and walk the island paths for views of the city, surrounding islands, and the ships in the Gulf of Finland. In the evening, treat yourself to dinner in one of Helsinki's restaurants specialising in local ingredients. Then hit the streets around Fredrikinkatu to learn what real nightlife is.

2–3 DAYS: TIME TO SEE MUCH MORE

You can fit a lot more in if you have another day or two. The first stop should be the Design Museum (see page 71), after which you will want to wander in the exciting Design District Helsinki to see what's at the cutting edge before it hits the shops all over Europe. Don't miss the Design Forum (see page 79), where you can find top designers' work to suit all budgets. Window-shop your way north along Fredrikinkatu or take a bus to Temppeliaukio Church (see page 91), carved out of solid rock. Head back east towards the unmissable tower of the National Museum (see page 75) and Finlandia Hall (see page 73), opposite, before returning to the centre along busy Mannerheimintie. If you have another day, spend it visiting some of the other excellent museums or head for the islands: either the open-air museum of Seurasaari (see page 114) or the Korkeasaari Zoo (see page 109) to see rare big cats, including snow leopards and Siberian tigers.

LONGER: ENJOYING HELSINKI TO THE FULL

A longer stay gives enough time to head out of the city for a day in old Porvoo or for one of the many cruises among the islands. Alternatively, combine the two by cruising to Porvoo. After pounding the pavements for a few days, you'll be ready to relax in one of Helsinki's parks, where you can snowshoe or ski in the winter and walk or cycle in the summer. After that, you'll be ready for the other Finnish obsession: the sauna. If your hotel doesn't offer one, choose one of the city's public saunas and join the Finns as they relax.

Something for nothing

Attending one of Helsinki's free festivals not only saves money, but it's also a great way to mingle with locals, enjoy music and be part of Finnish life. However, since the majority take place during the highest tourism season, you'll need to book accommodation early.

The ultimate in syncretism is the confluence of Walpurgis Night (itself coinciding with the pagan rites of spring), May Day, International Workers' Day and Finland's Student Day (celebrating

◯ *Students crowd into Senate Square to celebrate Student Day*

graduation). The city welcomes spring (even if the day brings a late snowstorm) in a most un-Finnish way, by becoming one giant block party, with champagne, picnics and bands of liberated students wearing white hats. A cap is placed ceremoniously on the statue of Havis Amanda on the evening of 30 April, and champagne flows – along with goodwill – well into the night and all the next day.

The last weekend in May brings the **World Village Festival** (Ⓦ www.maailmakylassa.fi), two days of free stage performances, exhibitions, street musicians and sports in Kaisaniemi Park. Several stages feature performers from all over the world, many of them emerging artists that go on to become famous. Past performances have included Senegalese hip hop, Chilean reggae, Finnish folk rock and a Spanish ska/rock/flamenco/Raï group. Exotic food, folk crafts and exhibition booths add to the atmosphere, with an international buzz filling the city.

Helsinki-päivä, Helsinki Day, celebrates the city's birthday on 12 June, with free concerts, a three-day samba and dance festival with cruises, tours and free entrance to museums. It ends with a rock concert in Kaivopuisto Park, (close to the British and United States embassies, off Puistokatu). There are market stalls on Esplanadi, free performances on the Espa stage all day and free admission to Suomenlinna Fortress. It is especially good for families with children, as it is relatively alcohol-free.

Most summer weekends bring Alppipuisto (next to the Linnanmäki Amusement Park) alive with music, free of charge. For a week in mid-August, the Art Goes Kapakka festival also offers a wide range of free entertainment in the bars of Helsinki. Night of the Arts takes place on a Friday in late August, with museums and galleries staying open until late at night and the streets coming alive with free musical performances.

When it rains

Helsinki is such an outdoor city, filled with leafy parks, broad avenues, street markets and pedestrianised shopping streets, that most travellers spend much of their time outside enjoying the long daylight hours. Three of its most famous sights – Suomenlinna Fortress, Seurasaari and Korkeasaari Zoo – are open-air attractions. But a whole layer of the city is so hidden that even multi-time visitors might not know it exists under their feet. Beneath the streets of the city centre, from the railway station to Esplanadi, under Mannerheimintie to the Forum shopping centre, and as far west as the Kamppi bus station, lies a maze of connected underground passages lined with shops, cafés, restaurants, bakeries and food markets. Street musicians play, and escalators and stairs connect to the department stores, shopping centres and services above.

The tunnels even offer direct access to transportation, connecting the train and bus stations and city transit lines. In cold or rainy weather you can spend a whole day shopping or browsing in the subterranean shops, the department stores of Stockmann and Sokos, the trendy shops of the Forum and Kamppi shopping centres, and even the Academic Bookstore, without ever emerging above ground.

The two department stores and the Forum have their food stores on the subterranean level, which are better places to look for typical foods than in the tourist shops. Browse the shelves for wild berry preserves and the fridges for smoked fish and venison. Both departments stores have good sections for Finnish design, in both fashion and home furnishings, as well as sections for typical local products, including genuine Sámi-made goods. The Kamppi shopping centre offers designer shops and a variety of restaurants and cafés. If you are feeling adventurous, take the eastbound metro from the train station to Itäkeskus, where you'll find a huge shopping centre.

The underground routes access at least two of Helsinki's architectural landmarks, the interior of Eliel Saarinen's railway station and the Academic Bookstore, designed by Alvar Aalto. And close to their exits are two art museums well worth exploring on a rainy day: the **Ateneum** (see page 71), with the country's best collections of Finnish and foreign art, and **Kiasma Museum of Contemporary Art** (see page 74), featuring post-1960 Finnish works. (Without the visible landmarks of the world above, it is easy to lose your bearings in the tunnels, so signs help you find your way.)

🔺 *The Academic Bookstore is a destination in its own right*

On arrival

TIME DIFFERENCE

Helsinki follows Eastern European Time (EET), two hours ahead of GMT. During Daylight Saving Time (end Mar–end Oct) the clocks are put forward one hour.

ARRIVING

By air

Helsinki-Vantaa International Airport (ⓣ 0200 14636 ⓦ www.helsinki-vantaa.fi) is 19 km (12 miles) north of the city centre. The two-terminal (domestic and international) airport has three shopping centres and numerous bureaux de change and ATMs. Finnair operates a shuttle to Helsinki Railway Station, leaving every 20–30 minutes between 05.00 and 24.00 and costing €6.20 for the 30-minute journey. Public buses take around 40 minutes to reach the station but cost slightly less (€4) and depart every 10–30 minutes between 05.00 and 03.00. Taxis deliver you and your luggage directly to your hotel for about €40–45.

An alternative gateway used by low-cost airlines such as Ryanair is **Tampere-Pirkkala Airport** (ⓣ 20 708 5311 ⓦ www.finavia.fi), usually known as Tampere. Bus timetables are linked to arrival times with the shuttles going direct to Helsinki Railway Station; the one-way fare is €25 and the journey time 2½ hours.

By rail

Rail passengers arrive at one of Helsinki's great architectural landmarks, Eliel Saarinen's 1911 granite **Helsingin rautatieasema** (Helsinki Railway Station ⓐ Kaivokatu 1 ⓣ 0600 41 902 ⓦ www.vr.fi). This busy terminus has a wealth of facilities – including restaurants and coffee shops, ATMs, public card phones and its own shopping centre – and is right in the centre of the city. Unlike many other large European stations, it is located in a busy, safe and upmarket area.

By road

Coach services arrive at the high-tech underground **Kamppi station** (ⓐ Narinkka 3 ⓣ 0200 4000 ⓦ www.matkahuolto.fi). Finnish buses and coaches are reliable and comfortable and get you to places where trains do not go.

In Helsinki, traffic is light, roads are well marked (and free of tolls) and drivers polite. But unless you plan to travel outside the capital and into the countryside, a car is really not necessary because the public transport is so good.

If you are from a left-hand-drive country, be especially aware that in Finland driving is on the right, and cars overtake on the left. Drivers bringing their own cars from the UK should be sure their lights are adapted to right-hand driving. Drivers from outside the EU should carry an International Driving Permit (available from local automobile clubs before leaving home), along with their national licence. Unless otherwise posted, the speed limit is 80 km/h (50 mph) outside the city, 50 km/h (30 mph) within the city limits and 100–120 km/h (60–75 mph) on motorways (the limit increases with the number of lanes). In the city, trams, bicycles and pedestrians have right of way over cars. Seat belts are compulsory everywhere.

If you intend to travel by car in the winter, you should be familiar with handling a vehicle on snow-covered and icy roads and driving in winter storm conditions. Winter wheels are mandatory on every car between November and March. Anywhere outside the city, be aware that reindeer and elk are formidable obstacles that can appear suddenly on the road at any time. Hundreds of people are

Seurasaari

Humallahti

PASUKSENKATU
FENRIKSSONAN
LINNANKOSKENKATU
TORELIUSGATAN
MECKANGATAN
TÖLEGSGATAN

Olympiastadion

MANNERHEIMINTIE

HELSINGINKATU

Kaupungin
Talvipuutarha

Linnann
Amusen
Park

Sibelius-
monumentti

TAKA-TÖÖLÖ

Suomen
Kansallisooppera

Sibelius
Park

Töölönlahti

Taivallahti

POHJOINEN   HESPERIANKATU

ETELÄINEN   HESPERIANKATU

MECHELININKATU

RUNEBERGINKATU

MANNERHEIMINTIE

Suomen
kansallismuseo

MUSEOKATU

Finlandia-
talo

Musiikkitalo

Hietaniemi
hautausmaa

HIEKKARANNANTIE

SANDUDDSGATAN

TEMPPELIKATU

Temppelaukion
kirkko

Parliament
House

Taidehalli

ARKADIANKATU

Kiasr
nyky
muse

Helsingi
rautatieasem
Rautatietor

Lapinlahti

ETU-
TÖÖLÖ

RUNEBERGINKATU

POHJOINEN

ETELÄINEN

YRJÖNKATU

KALEVANKATU

Lasipalatsi

Amos Andersonin
taidemuseo
Kampin

Forur
Shop
Cen

Kampti Bus
Station &
Shopping Centre

LAPINLAHDENKATU

KAMPPI

FREDRIKINKATU

KALEVANKA

LÄNSIVÄYLÄ

VÄSTERLEDEN

RUOHOLAHDENKATU

EERIKINKATU
KALEVAGATAN

LÖNNROTINKATU

LÖNNROTSGATAN

BULEVARDI

UUDENMAA

LÖNNROTIN

PORKKALANKATU

ITÄMERENKATU
ÖSTERSJÖGATAN

HIETALAHDENRANTA

Sinebrychoffin
taidemuseo

PUNAVUORI

PUNAVUOREN

Kaapelitehdas

Ruoholahti

RUOHOLAHTI

JAVAKSANKATU
SKYBBICKSGATAN

Hietalahti

TELAKKAKATU

PURJE

Lauttasaarensalmi

HERSARINKUJA

Helsingin
automuseo

FABRIKSGATA

EIR

MERIKATU

West
Terminal

HAVSSTRÄNDEN

Helsinki

0   500 metres
0   500 yards

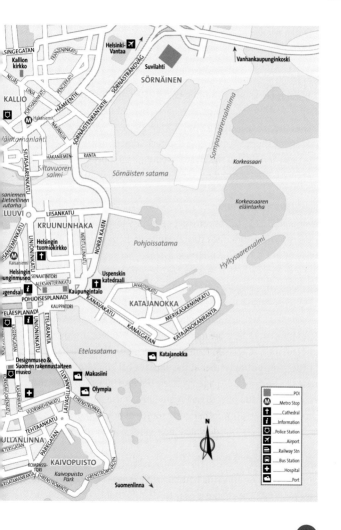

killed in wildlife collisions annually, so slow down whenever you see one, and be especially careful at dusk or in the dark.

By sea

The three ferry and cruise ship docks – Olympia Terminal, Makasiini Terminal and Katajanokka Terminal – are right in the centre of the city in the South Harbour, within a few steps of the market, Esplanadi, shopping streets and hotels. Some services arrive at the West Terminal in the West Harbour just a short bus ride from the centre. For information, see Ⓦ www.portofhelsinki.fi

FINDING YOUR FEET

Few capital cities are as compact or as easy to get around as Helsinki. The central sites surround the harbour, and the city is laid out in a tidy grid with broad avenues. Some of Helsinki's most outstanding architecture is visible from the harbour, and its streets are lined with elegant old buildings. The city is clean, well lit and safe, with drivers who are mindful of pedestrians.

The neat, sensible street plan makes finding addresses easy (and house numbers are marked on most local maps), although street names may seem to defy pronunciation. Pick up a free map at the tourist office, either at the airport or at Pohjoisesplanadi 19, near the harbour (see page 153). Here you can buy a Helsinki Card, economical if you plan to visit many sites or use public transport often (see page 58). Another great source of neighbourhood maps is *See Helsinki on Foot*, downloadable via Ⓦ www.visithelsinki.fi

ORIENTATION

The city wraps around the harbour, with Senate Square behind it (see page 68). The square is easy to identify thanks to the round

IF YOU GET LOST, TRY ...

Excuse me, do you speak English?
Anteeksi, puhutko englantia?
Erntehksi, puhutko ehnglerntier?

How do I get to ...?
Miten mä pääsen ...?
Miten mah pa-a-sen ...?

Can you show me on my map?
Voitko näyttää mulle kartasta?
Voytko na-ewtta-a mulleh kerterster?

dome of the Lutheran Cathedral. To the east the golden domes of
Uspenski Cathedral (see page 70), on a second hill, provide another
useful landmark, and to the west stretches Esplanadi (see page 64), a
wide park bordered by elegant buildings. From the end of Esplanadi,
the broad Mannerheimintie heads northwest, alongside the railway
station and Töölönlahti. Between these are the unmistakable
Finlandia Hall and the new Musiikkitalo (see page 73), and a bit
further up is the National Opera (see page 75). The **Parliament
House** (❸ Mannerheimintie 30) and the tall tower of the National
Museum of Finland (see page 75) are the main landmarks on
Mannerheimintie's western side.

From this walkable nucleus, other neighbourhoods are easy
to find: the *Jugendstil* Katajanokka lies east beyond Uspenski
Cathedral, Kallio north of Senate Square, Hietaniemi to the west,

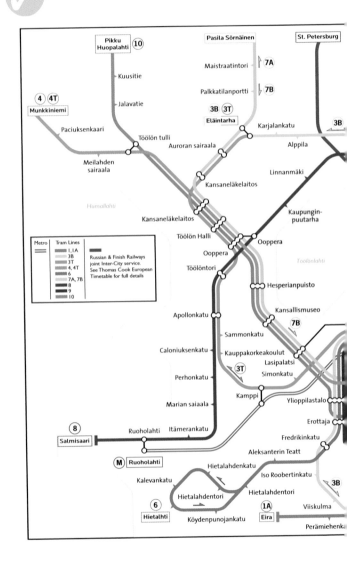

Sibelius Park to the northwest, Bulevardi to the south as are the neighbourhoods and parks of the southern end of the peninsula. The three main islands – Seurasaari, Suomenlinna and Korkeasaari – are respectively west, southeast and east of the city. The handy website ⓦ http://kartta.hel.fi will help you locate any street address.

GETTING AROUND

Buses, trams and a single metro line make getting around Helsinki easy. The website ⓦ www.hsl.fi has general information plus a journey planner giving exact public transport connections between any two points, including scheduled times. Tickets can be purchased in advance from machines at stations and are valid on all forms of land-based transport in the city. If you expect to use public transport often, a tourist ticket allowing unlimited use of the system costs €7 for 24 hours, €14 for three days and €21 for five days. Otherwise, single tickets cost €2 and allow transfers within the hour. You can also buy a slightly cheaper tram-only single ticket for €1.80 (from machines). Bus drivers do sell single tickets, but these are more expensive at €2.50.

Another option is the Helsinki Card (one day €35, two days €45, three days €55), which also includes free admission to museums and attractions. This is only good value, however, if you plan to visit several attractions, since admission fees to most major sights are around €5–8. Entrance to all the separate museums on Suomenlinna plus the ferry trip adds up to more than a 24-hour Helsinki Card, but that assumes that you would tour every little museum in the complex.

Ferries shuttle continuously between the harbour and Suomenlinna (€4 return) and a little less frequently to Korkeasaari Zoo from the harbour or Hakaniemenranta.

Hail taxis from the street (the yellow sign will be lit if it is available), or at busy times go to a taxi rank or phone ⓣ 0100 0700. The base rate is €5.30, or €8.30 at night and weekends. A journey to most city destinations will cost €8–12. Tipping is not necessary, but if you do, add €1 to the fare.

In good weather, cycling is a great way to get around. The city is relatively flat, with over 900 km (560 miles) of cycle lanes and paths following the main streets. Some hotels have bikes for guests' use, or you can rent from **Greenbike** (① 50 550 1020 Ⓦ www.greenbike.fi).

If you're thinking of travelling further afield, you'll have to take a train, plane or coach. Getting around Finland is easy and efficient

⬢ A tram in Senate Square, just below the Lutheran cathedral

using buses, trains or internal flights, but it can be expensive unless you fall into one of the discount groups. The fastest trains are the Pendolinos, connecting major destinations such as Helsinki and Turku. Express trains go to northern cities such as Rovaniemi in Lapland, which is an 11-hour journey. InterRail, Eurail and other passes are valid in Finland (see page 143). Bus services are scheduled to be compatible with trains, reaching out into the countryside and smaller towns. Finnair flies to Rovaniemi and other northern outposts.

Bus information ⓘ 0200 4000 Ⓦ www.matkahuolto.fi or the **journey planner** Ⓦ www.journey.fi

Finnair ⓘ 0600 140 140 Ⓦ www.finnair.com

Train information ⓘ 0600 41 902 Ⓦ www.vr.fi

Car hire

All major companies are represented in Helsinki, most with desks at Helsinki-Vantaa Airport. Check car-hire rates before making air reservations, since you can often save with an air car package from the airline.

If you plan to visit Helsinki before travelling elsewhere, consider picking up the car as you leave, instead of on arrival, to save city driving and parking charges. The minimum age for car hire is 18, and you must present (and carry while driving) your own home driving licence. Non-EU residents should also have an International Driving Permit, obtained from an automobile club (you needn't be a member) before leaving home. In addition, you will need to show a credit card, even if you are not charging the car to one. If you plan to take the car on the ferry to Estonia or Sweden, be sure you have the necessary documentation (you should ask for this when you book).

◐ *Helsinki Railway Station*

THE CITY OF
Helsinki

Esplanadi & the harbour

So many of Helsinki's most popular sights are in the streets surrounding the harbour that it would be easy to spend several days in this area without venturing any further. Outstanding architecture, churches, museums, dining and shopping are all within a few steps of the busy waterfront, which, given the number of ships and boats that seem to be constantly moving in and out, is itself a scenic attraction.

SIGHTS & ATTRACTIONS

Half the fun of visiting Helsinki is the variety of sights and experiences. High on that list is just ambling around the harbour and through the city's markets, enjoying the architecture and the constantly changing waterscape. Each time you approach the harbour, it looks different, as the huge Baltic ferries and cruise ships come and go, and little boats sail in and out.

Design District Helsinki

The area around Diana Park is full of design and antique shops, fashion stores, museums, art galleries, restaurants and showrooms. Here you can find fascinating examples of the work of the people who really matter. For an immediate immersion into the aesthetic that governs Finnish design, one could do a lot worse than to pay a visit to this area. Guided walking tours of the Design District Helsinki are organised by the company Helsinki Expert (see page 36). Walks start from the Esplanade Park on Mondays and Fridays at 13.30. For an up-to-date list of participating venues and artists, check ⓦ www.designdistrict.fi

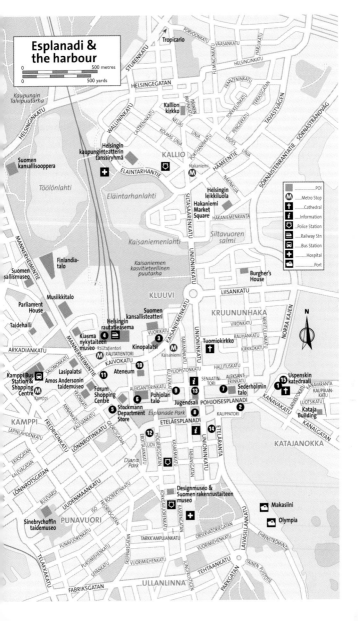

Esplanadi

Stretching west from Kauppatori (Market Square), the open
swathe of Esplanadi is bordered by elegant buildings. Two
streets make up Esplanadi: Eteläesplanadi and, slightly to the north,
Pohjoisesplanadi. The pavilion at the beginning of the park is the
Café Kappeli, and the nearby bandstand is the scene of free

JUGENDSTIL

At the turn of the 20th century, a unique combination of events,
ideas and talents propelled Finland and its capital city into the
spotlight of European design. Finland's rising intellectual and
artistic community, already seeking its own national identity
(see page 14), was further inspired by the Arts and Crafts
movement popular in Europe at the time. Today, the results
of that golden age of Finnish Art make Helsinki a living
museum of *Jugendstil*, as Art Nouveau was known in German-
speaking countries.

The primary architects were Lars Sonck, Sigurd Frosterus,
Selim Lindqvist, Valter Thomé, Herman Gesellius, Armas Lindgren
and Eliel Saarinen. Helsinki was in a rapid growth spurt, so housing
and public buildings were in great demand – and so were these
brilliant young architects to design them. Dozens of their
landmark buildings cluster in easy-to-visit neighbourhoods.

One of Europe's signature buildings in this style is
Saarinen's Helsinki Railway Station, dramatic straight lines
accented by four giant granite figures by Emil Wikström. The
interior is a triumph of *Jugendstil*, with its combination of

summer concerts. Before Christmas, the entire Esplanadi is lined with booths selling crafts and food. Between it and Market Square, a statue of Helsinki's symbol, Havis Amanda, emerges from a fountain. The fountain is the work of Eliel Saarinen, and *Havis Amanda* is by Ville Vallgren. Esplanade Park, between the two streets, is filled with strollers on summer evenings.

an elegantly simple structure with flowing lines of natural ornamental designs.

Nearby streets boast several other noteworthy structures – you can't miss the rusticated stone exterior of the Pohjola Insurance Building at Aleksanterinkatu 44 (see page 68). Its interior, mixing stone with local wood, features designs of native plants and animals. Climb the stairs to see *Jugendstil* balustrades, doors, hinges, panels, and even a newel post.

Just beyond the Uspenski Cathedral (see page 70) are some of the city's best residential examples of the style. Katajanokka (see page 67) was the first neighbourhood of this type in Europe, and is also Europe's best preserved. Wander the streets of this quarter, looking for details of stone ornament as well as surprising doorways, fanciful hinges, fairytale towers, balconies and other architectural details.

To see the best of Helsinki's *Jugendstil*, sign up for the 'Inside Helsinki' tour with Archtours. Architect Marianna Heikinheimo or one of her associates will take you to a wide range of sites, including the city's best examples of *Jugendstil*. **Archtours** ❶ 09 477 7300 ❿ www.archtours.fi

Helsingin leikkiluola (Helsinki Playground)

A great place for families on a rainy day. You have two hours
(🕙 10.00–12.00, 12.00–14.00 up to 18.00–20.00) to make full use of
the bouncy castles, trampolines and Lego. There's plenty on offer for
children of all ages. 🅐 Jaffa Station, Sörnäisten rantatie 6, at
Hakaniemi Market Square 📞 020 710 9902 🌐 www.leikkiluola.fi
🕙 10.00–20.00 daily 🔵 Metro: Hakaniemi; tram: 1A, 3B, 6, 7B, 8, 9
ⓘ Admission charge for children; parents free

Helsingin rautatieasema (Helsinki Railway Station)

For visitors arriving by rail or airport bus, the first stop is Helsinki's
Jugendstil railway station, designed by Eliel Saarinen. Its tower is said
to have influenced America's first generation of skyscrapers,
including the 1929 Gulf Building in Houston, Texas, now owned
by JPMorgan Chase. Be sure to go inside to see the monumental
arched halls, with walls decorated with surprisingly delicate carved
panels. 🅐 Rautatientori 🔵 Metro: Rautatientori

Jugendsali (Jugend Hall)

Jugendstil meets medieval in this 1904 interior by architect Lars Sonck.
Romanesque churches seem to have inspired the banking hall's low
vaulting and three 'naves', but the similarities end there. Sonck uses
the stone itself as a decorative material, sometimes rough-surfaced
and rusticated, or polished to a high gloss in the muscular pillars.
Relief carvings in their capitals are reminiscent of Viking ship prows, a
popular Scandinavian theme but not frequently seen in Finland. Today,
the hall serves as a café and hosts the occasional concert and art
exhibition as well. 🅐 Pohjoisesplanadi 19 📞 09 3101 3800
🕙 09.00–17.00 Mon–Fri, 11.00–17.00 Sun, closed Sat (Aug–June);
09.00–16.00 Mon–Fri, closed Sat & Sun (July) 🔵 Tram: 1A, 3T

Kaisaniemen kasvitieteellinen puutarha (Kaisaniemi Botanical Gardens)

The iron-framed glass Palm House was designed by Gustaf Nystrom in 1889, and today more than 900 labelled plant species grow in rainforest, desert, Mediterranean and water environments. Go in the winter to be among orchids, African violets and water lilies with massive leaves. The flowerbeds, fountains, pools and rose borders are beautiful in June. ⓐ Enter from Unioninkatu 44 or Kaisaniemenranta 2, near the railway station ⓣ 09 1912 4453 ⓛ Gardens: 09.00–20.00 daily (Apr–Sept); 09.00–17.00 daily (Oct–Mar); glasshouses: 10.00–17.00 Tues–Sun, closed Mon (Apr–Sept); 10.00–15.00 Tues–Sun, closed Mon (Oct–Mar) ⓘ Admission charge to glasshouses

Kallion kirkko (Kallio Church)

One of Finland's great architects, Lars Sonck, designed this great church in the National Romantic style in 1912. The bells inside its distinctive tower play a piece by Sibelius. Go inside the granite building to see the sculpted relief and other works of art, and go for a Sunday service or a concert to hear the great organs. ⓐ Itäinen Papinkatu 2 ⓣ 09 2340 3620 ⓛ 12.00–17.00 Mon–Fri, 10.00–18.00 Sat & Sun ⓝ Tram: 1A, 3B, 9

Katajanokka

The city's best concentration of *Jugendstil* architecture can be found in the streets beyond the Uspenski Cathedral, across the harbour from Market Square. Built within a decade, at the height of *Jugendstil*'s popularity, this is Europe's best preserved *Jugendstil* residential neighbourhood. Each new apartment building, for the wealthy middle class who could afford quality design and construction, was designed to outdo its neighbours. The castle-like Aeolus building and the turreted Tallbergin talo, across the street, form a gate to the quarter, at either side of Luotsikatu, which is lined with fine examples. Behind Tallbergin is another signature building, Eol, with a projecting balcony, corner turret and outstanding wooden door with elegant iron fittings and carved mythic creatures. The most exquisite doorway, however, is on the 1902 **Kataja building** (Ⓐ Kaupiaankatu 2 Ⓝ Tram: 4T).

Kauppatori (Market Square) & Kauppahalli (Market Hall)

At the harbour's edge, with some of its merchants selling directly from boats, is the colourful market, a daily gathering of locals, visitors and traders. Impromptu cafés, enclosed by plastic in the winter, serve everything from juicy sausages to salmon grilled on cedar planks. At the Esplanadi side of the harbour is Gustaf Nystrom's 1889 market, worth visiting for the stalls of honey, smoked fish, local cheese and other delicacies. Ⓐ Helsinki harbour Ⓛ Indoor market: 08.00–18.00 Mon–Fri, 08.00–16.00 Sat; outdoor market: 06.30–18.00 Mon–Fri, 06.30–16.00 Sat (also 10.00–16.00 Sun in summer) Ⓝ Tram: 1A, 3T

Pohjolan talo (Pohjola Insurance Building)

The interior motifs used in this 1901 office building by Saarinen, Lindgren & Gesellius are clearly Finnish, but the style shows the influence of French *Jugendstil*. The dramatic sweeping staircase is asymmetrical, bordered with graceful balustrades. *Jugendstil* elements decorate these, as well as the walls and doorways of each landing. To see the interior, go during weekday business hours, wait until someone opens the door and simply walk in. Ⓐ Aleksanterinkatu 44 Ⓝ Tram: 3B, 3T, 4T, 7A/B

Senaatintori & Tuomiokirkko (Senate Square & Lutheran Cathedral)

Up the hill behind the market, its dome visible above the row of intervening buildings, the majestic neoclassical Lutheran Cathedral

⬤ *Katajanokka is an outdoor museum of* Jugendstil *domestic architecture*

is the focal point of Senate Square. The buildings at its adjoining sides, also by C L Engel, create an unusually unified public space – and one of Europe's finest squares. It's a well used one, too, for celebrations that range from Finland's Independence Day to the start of the St Lucia Parade before Christmas. The early 19th-century cathedral, with its tall green dome, stands high above the square, at the top of a long flight of steps. Sederholm House, the oldest stone building in Helsinki, faces the lower corner of the square. ⓐ Intersection of Unioninkatu and Aleksanterinkatu streets ① 09 2340 6120 ② Cathedral: 09.00–24.00 daily (summer); 09.00–18.00 daily (winter) Ⓝ Tram: 1A, 3T, 4T, 7A/B

Tropicario

This is the most modern and exciting tropical terrarium in the Nordic countries. It boasts fantastic examples of some amazing flora and fauna, including crocodiles, snakes and lizards of all types, with which you can interact up close and personal. This plot of Finnish jungle really isn't one for the phobic, but everybody else will have a roaring good time. ⓐ Sturenkatu 27 ① 09 750 076 Ⓦ www.tropicario.com ② 10.00–19.00 daily Ⓝ Tram: 1A, 7B

Uspenskin katedraali (Uspenski Cathedral)

Dominating the far side of the harbour is western Europe's largest Orthodox church, an ornate brick pile whose dome and towers are crowned by 13 gold cupolas. The interior is a wondrous cavern of icons, crosses, altars and gleaming gold, its intricately decorated arches offset by black marble columns. Along with serving the local Orthodox and Russian population, the church marks Helsinki's long-standing Russian influence. ⓐ Kanavakatu 1 ① 020 7220 683 ② 09.30–16.00 Mon–Fri, 09.30–14.00 Sat, 12.00–15.00 Sun

(May–Sept); 09.30–16.00 Tues–Fri, 09.30–14.00 Sat, 12.00–15.00 Sun, closed Mon (Oct–Apr) 🚊 Tram: 4T

CULTURE

A high concentration of the city's many museums lies in this central area; all are within easy walking distance of each other. The Helsinki Card admits visitors to nearly all of these museums, as well as to other attractions.

Amos Andersonin taidemuseo (Amos Anderson Art Museum)

This features mainly 20th-century Finnish art and furnishings from Amos Anderson's private collections. There is also Finnish and foreign art from the collection of the architect Sigurd Frosterus. As one would expect, both exhibit excellent taste. Watch out for special exhibitions. 📍 Yrjönkatu 27 📞 09 684 4460 🌐 www.amosanderson.fi 🕐 10.00–18.00 Mon, Thur & Fri, 10.00–20.00 Wed, 11.00–17.00 Sat & Sun, closed Tues 🚇 Metro: Rautatientori; tram: 3T ❶ Admission charge

Ateneum

The building is a beautiful setting for Finnish painting, sculpture, graphics and drawings, as well as international art. It includes works by artists such as Akseli Gallen-Kallela which are true national treasures. 📍 Kaivokatu 2 (opposite railway station) 📞 09 1733 6401 🌐 www.ateneum.fi 🕐 10.00–18.00 Tues & Fri, 10.00–20.00 Wed & Thur, 11.00–17.00 Sat & Sun, closed Mon 🚇 Metro: Rautatientori ❶ Admission charge

Designmuseo (Design Museum)

Nowhere is the evolution of decorative styles better illustrated than in the ground-floor gallery of the Design Museum. Decorative arts in ceramics, glass, metal, fabrics, furniture, utensils and décor show how various style periods interpreted these items. So if you are unclear about just how Victorian gave way to *Jugendstil* and how that morphed into Art Deco and modernism, you can see side-by-side examples. Although the primary focus is on Finnish design, special exhibitions may feature other designers or themes. The shop is a treasure box of quality design gifts and books. ❸ Korkeavuorenkatu 23 ❶ 09 622 0540 ⓦ www.designmuseo.fi ⏰ 11.00–18.00 daily (June–Aug); 11.00–20.00 Tues, 11.00–18.00 Wed–Sun, closed Mon (Sept–May) Ⓝ Tram: 10; bus: 16 ❶ Admission charge

🔽 *Finlandia-talo, the National Museum and Musiikkitalo rising above Töölönlahti*

Finlandia-talo (Finlandia Hall)

Completed in 1971, famed architect Alvar Aalto's best-known work in Helsinki is the graceful marble-clad concert hall overlooking Töölönlahti. Its primacy as a concert venue has recently been usurped by the new Musiikkitalo, and Finlandia-talo is now more often used as a congress and meeting centre, albeit a unique one. Tours of the landmark building take place on Wednesday afternoons, when other events allow. A new extension (Veranda) includes a café as well as new facilities for meetings and exhibitions. ⓐ Mannerheimintie 13 E ⓣ 09 40 241 ⓦ www. finlandiatalo.fi ⓥ 4, 4T, 7A, 7B, 10 ⓘ Admission charge for tours

Helsingin kaupunginteatterin tanssiryhmä (Helsinki Contemporary Dance Theatre)

Finland's largest modern dance ensemble, with a busy programme of performances. ⓐ Eläintarhantie 5, in Hakaniemi ⓣ 09 394 022 ⓦ www.hkt.fi ⓛ Box office: 09.00–18.00 Mon–Fri ⓜ Metro: Hakaniemi; tram: 1A, 3B, 6, 7, 9. Tickets also available from ⓐ Eerikinkatu 2 ⓛ 09.00–19.00 Mon–Fri, 12.00–19.00 Sat, closed Sun

Kiasma nykytaiteen museo (Kiasma Museum of Contemporary Art)

The home of Finnish modern art is, like the city's other art museums, as much about the building as its contents. Designed by the American architect Steven Holl, the curvy Kiasma opened in 1998, and is considered one of Finland's paramount works of modern architecture – no small feat in the native land of so many well-known architects. It contains a theatre for experimental drama, dance and music, as well as collections of post-1960 Finnish art. ⓐ Mannerheiminaukio 2 ⓣ 09 1733 6501 ⓦ www.kiasma.fi ⓛ 10.00–17.00 Tues, 10.00–20.30 Wed–Thur, 10.00–20.00 Fri, 10.00–17.00 Sat & Sun, closed Mon ⓜ Metro: Rautatientori; tram: 4T, 7, 10 ⓘ Admission charge

Musiikkitalo (Helsinki Music Centre)

Opened in August 2011, Musiikkitalo is now home to both the Helsinki Philharmonic Orchestra and the Finnish Radio Symphony Orchestra, as well as the Sibelius Academy music school. The striking building fills a once forlorn space opposite Parliament House and hosts an eclectic range of concerts – folk, jazz and rock as well as classical. In its opening year, tours of the building have proved extremely popular, so enquire well in advance. ⓐ Mannerheimintie 13A ⓣ 020 707 0405 ⓦ www.musiikkitalo.fi ⓜ Metro: Rautatientori; tram: 4T, 7, 10 ⓘ Admission charge for tours

Sederholmin talo (Sederholm House)

Overlooking Senate Square, this is the central city's oldest stone building (built in 1757). It contains exhibitions from various city museums. Aleksanterinkatu 16–18 09 3103 6529 11.00–17.00 Wed–Sun (until 19.00 Thur), closed Mon & Tues Bus/tram: 1, 3T, 3B, 4 Admission charge

Suomen kansallismuseo (National Museum of Finland)

Your first stop to learn about Finnish culture and traditions, the museum also covers Finland's history from prehistoric times to the present. Historical artefacts and ethnographic collections illustrate daily life as well as events. Like the Ateneum, the building itself is a landmark, designed by the pre-eminent firm of Saarinen, Lindgren & Gesellius in 1902. Mannerheimintie 34 09 4050 9544 www.nba.fi 11.00–20.00 Tues, 11.00–18.00 Wed–Sun, closed Mon Bus/tram: 4, 4T, 7, 10 Admission charge

Suomen kansallisooppera (National Opera)

This modern stage is among Europe's finest, with a revolving floor, flexible mirrored ceiling and other techno tricks. Behind-the-scene tours are offered on Wednesdays at 14.30, but are only given in Finnish. Tickets begin as low as €12, and some performances are free. As well as offering around a dozen opera productions a year, the theatre hosts performances by the Suomen kansallisbaletti (National Ballet). Helsinginkatu 58 09 4030 21 www.opera.fi/en Box office: 09.00–18.00 Mon–Fri, 15.00–18.00 Sat Tram: 3T, 4T, 7, 8, 10

Suomen kansallisteatteri (National Theatre)

The focal point of the north side of the Helsinki Railway Station Square is the National Theatre, built in 1902, with a granite and

CHRISTMAS MARKETS

Every Finnish school child knows that Santa lives in Finland, just north of Rovaniemi, on the Arctic Circle. Many have even visited him there. The village where he lives with his elves and reindeer, is open all year, except 24 December, but you don't have to go all the way to the Arctic Circle to find the Finns celebrating the Christmas season.

It begins early in December with the Christmas market that springs up like a little village on Esplanadi. Helsinki's St Thomas Market forms a double row of bright tents, all outlined in tiny twinkling white lights. Step inside each one to find a tiny, brightly lit shop filled with beautiful handmade gifts: woodcarvings, knitted hats and mittens, gingerbread, wrought ironwork, fancy candles, woven scarves, wooden toys, fur hats, blown glass or jars of shimmering lingonberry jam.

sandstone façade. The interior is almost entirely worked in curved lines, while the foyer is decorated with frescoes. ❸ Suomen Kansallisteatteri, Läntinen Teatterikuja 1 Ⓦ www.kansallisteatteri.fi Ⓝ Metro: Rautatientori

Suomen rakennustaiteen museo (Museum of Finnish Architecture)
Special exhibitions highlight Finnish architects past and present, as well as the styles they created and influenced. The story of the museum building (100 years old and still not completed) is fascinating in itself. ❸ Kasarmikatu 24 ❶ 09 8567 5100 Ⓦ www. mfa.fi ⓛ 10.00–16.00 Tues, Thur & Fri, 10.00–20.00 Wed, 11.00–16.00 Sat & Sun, closed Mon Ⓝ Tram: 10; bus: 16 ❶ Admission charge

Brightly painted wooden puzzles come in shapes of fish, turtles, rabbits and hedgehogs. Velvet-smooth wooden cooking utensils – spatulas, forks, spoons and spreaders – are carved in graceful flowing shapes, from richly grained woods. Cups are formed from gnarly-grained tree burls, and cutting boards show off a variety of local woods in contrasting stripes. More rustic are the Christmas elves made of small angle-cut logs, with beards of curly yarn and peaked caps of bright felt. Smaller elves made of wool perch all around.

A warmer venue for a craft show is the **Women's Christmas Fair**, at Wanha Satama, across Helsinki's harbour (🕑 10.00–19.00, 2–6 Dec 🚊 Tram: 4, 4T). The variety is astonishing, from stacks of beeswax candles and creamy Finnish honey to elegant painted silks, hobby-horses, finger puppets, fashionable knitwear and cheery little red-hatted elves, all handmade.

RETAIL THERAPY

The Esplanadi and the streets north – Mannerheimintie, Aleksanterinkatu and Kaisaniemenkatu – are lined with the smartest shops, featuring the best in Finnish design. Just browsing their stunningly arranged windows is an art experience. On Senate Square and the streets around it you will find boutiques selling handicrafts and folk arts. In good weather, Market Square is filled with stalls selling craftworks and local produce. You could shop till you drop without leaving this small area of Helsinki – take trams 4, 6, 7A/B, 9 or 10 to get here and then explore on foot.

Aarikka Finland Clever, irresistible wooden creations, including Christmas decorations, home décor, jewellery and whimsical utensils. ⓐ Pohjoisesplanadi 27 ⓦ www.aarikka.fi ⓛ 09.00–19.00 Mon–Fri, 09.00–18.00 Sat, 12.00–18.00 Sun

Artek Furniture designed by Alvar Aalto forms the centrepiece, with other interior décor including rugs, linens, decorative fabrics and tableware. ⓐ Eteläesplanadi 18 ⓣ 09 617 3480 ⓛ 10.00–18.00 Mon–Fri, 10.00–16.00 Sat, closed Sun

◓ *The Design Forum is Finland's shop window to the world*

Craft Corner A stone's throw from the artisanal offerings of Kauppatori, this is home to three companies: OKRA, a collective of designer/makers; Arctic Pearls, which showcases crafts from Lapland; and Taito Shop Helsky, representing the Finnish Craft Organisation. **ⓐ** Eteläesplanadi 4 **ⓣ** 09 624 250 **ⓦ** www.okra.fi/craftcorner **ⓛ** 10.00–18.00 Mon–Fri, 10.00–16.00 Sat, closed Sun **ⓝ** Tram: 3T, 4, 4T, 7A, 7B

Design Forum To see – and buy – what's new and hot, shop at the Design Forum, where useful items from notebooks to kitchen appliances are practical as well as beautiful and stylish, affirming that Finnish design is among the best in the world. **ⓐ** Erottajankatu 7 **ⓣ** 09 6220 8130 **ⓦ** www.designforum.fi **ⓛ** 10.00–19.00 Mon–Fri, 12.00–17.00 Sat & Sun **ⓝ** Tram: 9, 10

Designers Gallery This is the place to be inspired by top-quality modern fashion for women as envisaged by prize-winning Finnish designers such as Iris Aalto, Ilona Pelli and Tarja Niskanen. **ⓐ** Kauppatori, Eteläesplanadi 4/Unioninkatu 26 **ⓣ** 050 340 8290 **ⓦ** www.designersgallery.fi **ⓛ** 10.00–18.00 Mon–Fri, 10.00–16.00 Sat, closed Sun **ⓝ** Tram: 1A, 3T

Marimeko® Famed for striking decorator fabrics, Marimeko® also leads the design world with tableware, bags and wearables. **ⓐ** Various locations include Pohjoisesplanadi 33, the Kamppi Shopping Centre & Urho Kekkosen katu 1 **ⓣ** 09 686 0240 **ⓦ** www.marimekko.com **ⓛ** Varies by store, so phone to check

Sokos Slightly less rarified than Stockmann, but with a wide variety of high-quality Finnish and Scandinavian goods, ranging from

fashions to furnishings. ➌ Mannerheimintie 9 ☏ 010 766 5100
🕐 09.00–21.00 Mon–Fri, 09.00–18.00 Sat; also open 12.00–21.00
Sun (summer & Dec)

Stockmann Even an entire city block, extended in 2010, can't hold all
the merchandise in the largest department store in the Nordic
countries. The stock overflows into the Academic Bookstore, across
Keskuskatu (and connected by a tunnel), in a building designed by
Alvar Aalto. ➌ Corner of Aleksanterinkatu and Mannerheimintie
Ⓦ www.stockmann.fi 🕐 09.00–21.00 Mon–Fri, 09.00–18.00 Sat,
12.00–18.00 Sun

TAKING A BREAK

Central Helsinki is filled with cafés, from elegant Old World
settings to cafés in shops, museums and even a ship in the harbour.
In the summer many of them move outdoors to enjoy the long
daylight hours.

Johan & Nystrom £ ❶ The Swedish coffee-roaster's concept store
in a Katajanokka warehouse has a small welcoming café near the
entrance serving the best Americano in Helsinki. ➌ Kanavaranta 7
☏ 0207 416 670 Ⓦ www.johanochnystrom.fi 🕐 07.30–18.00
Mon–Fri, 10.00–16.00 Sat, 12.00–16.00 Sun Ⓝ Tram: 4T; bus: 16

Kauppatorin Kahvila £ ❷ In a bright orange tent in the market, but
warm inside even on blustery snow-filled days, this is a favourite
of local politicos, who come for the coffee and the outstanding meat
pies. ➌ Kauppatori Ⓦ www.toripojat.fi 🕐 06.00–15.00 Mon–Fri,
06.00–16.00 Sat, 08.00–17.00 Sun Ⓝ Tram: 1, 3T, 4T, 7

Kipinä £ ❸ Unreserved atmosphere, cosy interior, excellent home-made food and friendly and professional service will guarantee an unforgettable time. ❸ Vuorikatu 16 ❶ 09 670 089 ⓦ www.ravintolakipina.fi ⏰ 11.00–24.00 Mon–Fri, 15.00–24.00 Sat, closed Sun Ⓝ Tram: 3B, 6, 9

Restaurant Eliel £ ❹ You might not normally choose a railway station for a meal, but this café is very popular with locals and visitors for good food and low prices. Breakfast is served until late morning, the buffet lunch until late afternoon; there's a full evening menu. ⓐ Rautatieasema ❶ 040 862 2965 ⏰ 07.30–23.00 Mon–Fri, 08.00–23.00 Sat, 10.00–22.00 Sun Ⓝ Metro: Rautatientori

Baker's Bar & Restaurant ££ ❺ Baker's is a versatile restaurant complex in the heart of Helsinki. On the international menu you'll find seasonal specialities as well as Finnish classics. During the week, a delicious buffet lunch is set from 11.00 till 14.00. A mouthwatering selection of different kinds of breads awaits all gourmets. ⓐ Mannerheimintie 12 ❶ 020 770 1440 ⓦ www.ravintolabakers.com ⏰ Restaurant: 11.00–22.00 Mon & Tues, 11.00–23.00 Wed–Fri, 13.00–23.00 Sat, closed Sun; café bar: 07.00–04.00 Mon–Fri, 10.00–04.00 Sat, 19.00–04.00 Sun Ⓝ Tram: 3B, 4T, 6, 8, 9, 10

Café Aalto ££ ❻ On the balcony of the Academic Bookstore, the café overlooks the shop's interior by Finnish design-meister Alvar Aalto. Relax with a book over coffee or have lunch here. The pastries are baked in-house. ⓐ Pohjoisesplanadi 39 ❶ 09 121 4446 ⓦ www.cafeaalto.fi ⏰ 09.00–19.00 Mon–Fri, 09.00–18.00 Sat; also open 12.00–19.00 Sun (summer & Dec) Ⓝ Tram: 3B, 3T, 4T, 6, 7, 9, 10

● *Café Kappeli – a landmark on Esplanadi*

Café Engel ££ ❼ In the dark days of a northern winter, this cheery café is brightly illuminated with 'daylight' bulbs. The coffee menu is long and the lingonberry pie is mouthwatering. ⓐ Aleksanterinkatu 26 ⓣ 09 652 776 ⓦ www.cafeengel.fi ⓛ 08.00–21.00 Mon–Fri, 09.00–21.00 Sat, 10.00–21.00 Sun ⓝ Tram: 1A, 3T, 4, 7

Café Kappeli ££ ❽ The café serves a soup lunch daily while the restaurant offers Finnish classics. Or you can just have a drink at the bar. ⓐ Eteläesplanadi 1 ⓣ 010 76 63880 ⓦ www.kappeli.fi ⓛ 09.00–24.00 daily ⓝ Tram: 1A, 3T, 4, 7

Karl Fazer Cafe ££ ❾ The venerable Fazer specialises in stunning sweet delicacies but a selection of soups, salads and pasta is also available most of the day. The breakfast buffet is the best in town and the desserts and chocolates are peerless. ⓐ Kluuvikatu 3 ⓣ 020 729 6702 ⓦ www.fazer.fi ⓛ 07.30–22.00 Mon–Fri, 09.00–22.00 Sat, closed Sun ⓝ Metro: Kaisaniemi; tram: 3T, 4T, 7

Tablo Ateneum ££ ❿ The café in the Ateneum museum has a daily changing lunch menu along with soups, pastries and cakes. ⓐ Rautatientori ❶ 09 1733 6231 ❶ 10.00–18.00 Tues & Fri, 11.00–20.00 Wed & Thur, 11.00–17.00 Sat & Sun, closed Mon Ⓜ Metro: Rautatientori; tram: 3B, 3T, 6, 9

AFTER DARK

Friday and Saturday are the big nights for partying, but Wednesday is also popular for clubs. Book ahead for dinner at the more sought-after restaurants in the city centre at weekends or in the summer.

RESTAURANTS

Virgin Oil Co. £–££ ⓫ By day and early evening, this is an excellent place for good-value wood-fired pizzas; upstairs is a lively club/bar for the later hours. ⓐ Mannerheimintie 5 ❶ 010 766 4000 Ⓦ www. virginoil.fi ❶ 11.00–24.00 Mon–Thur, 11.00–04.00 Fri, 12.00–04.00 Sat, 13.00–23.00 Sun Ⓜ Metro: Rautatientori; tram: 3B, 4T, 6, 8, 9, 10

Vespa ££ ⓬ Three Italian restaurants in one: a delicious upstairs ristorante, a busy street-level bar and deli and an atmospheric cellar trattoria. ⓐ Eteläesplanadi 22 ❶ 020 7701 466 Ⓦ www.ravintola vespa.fi ❶ Ristorante: 11.00–24.00 Mon, 12.00–24.00 Tues–Sat, closed Sun; bar & deli: 11.00–23.00 Mon, 11.00–24.00 Tues–Thur, 08.00–01.00 Fri, 12.00–24.00 Sat, closed Sun; trattoria: 17.00–24.00 Tues–Sat, closed Sun & Mon Ⓜ Tram: 3B, 6, 9, 10

Savotta ££–£££ ⓭ In a plum position on Senate Square and offering 'old-fashioned Finnish food and atmosphere', you might expect a fake, tacky tourist trap – but you would be wrong. Fittings and

tableware are genuine and so is the food, from the elk sirloin to the bewitchingly delicious *sisu* ice cream. ❸ Aleksanterinkatu 22
❶ 09 7425 5588 ❿ www.asrestaurants.com ◷ 12.00–23.00 Mon–Sat, 13.00–22.00 Sun ◎ Tram: 1, 3T, 4T, 7

G W Sundmans £££ ⓮ One of Finland's oldest restaurants, and still one of its best, Sundmans occupies a beautifully restored former mansion. *Jugendstil* interior details are soon forgotten as the food arrives, from the heavenly terrines with woodland mushrooms to the dessert of Arctic cloudberries. ❸ Eteläranta 16 (facing the harbour)
❶ 09 6128 5400 ❿ www.royalravintolat.com/sundmans ◷ 11.00–14.30, 17.00–24.00 Mon–Fri, 18.00–24.00 Sat, closed Sun ◎ Tram: 4, 7B

Sipuli £££ ⓯ The skylight looks straight up at the domes of the Uspenski Cathedral. Nordic ingredients from the sea and forest are elegantly prepared – a frothy pumpkin soup is sprinkled with roasted nuts, and fried scallops are paired with fennel purée and pomegranate vinaigrette. ❸ Kanavaranta 7 ❶ 09 6128 5500
❿ www.royalravintolat.com/sipuli ◷ 18.00–24.00 Tues–Sat, closed Sun ◎ Tram: 4T; bus: 16

BARS & CLUBS
Gaselli Patrons here can enjoy an extensive range of draught beers and bottled products. Finnish pop and rock is often played in this relaxed venue. ❸ Aleksanterinkatu 46 ❶ 09 8568 5800 ❿ www.rafla.fi/gaselli ◷ 16.00–24.00 Tues, 16.00–01.00 Wed–Thur, 16.00–03.00 Fri, 18.00–03.00 Sat, closed Sun & Mon ◎ Tram: 3T, 4T, 7

Hotel Kämp With around 100 varieties of wine sold by the glass, the bar in Hotel Kämp (see page 40) is the classiest place in town for a drink. Prices are surprisingly reasonable and there's a good brasserie and Japanese restaurant on-site as well. ⓐ Pohjoisesplanadi 29 ⓣ 09 5840 9530 ⓛ 10.00–01.00 Mon & Tues, 10.00–02.00 Wed–Fri, 11.00–02.00 Sat, 11.00–01.00 Sun ⓜ Metro: Kaisaniemi

Mecca This joint positively exudes soul, and the vast selection of cocktails only helps this spiritual dimension. There's a DJ from Wednesday to Saturday. ⓐ Korkeavuorenkatu 34 ⓣ 09 1345 6200 ⓦ www.mecca.fi ⓛ 17.00–24.00 Tues–Thur, 17.00–04.00 Fri & Sat; kitchen: 17.00–24.00 Tues–Sat, closed Sun & Mon ⓜ Tram: 9, 10; bus 42

Oluthoune Kaisla With a wide-ranging selection of draught beer and an even more eclectic bottled range, this is a setting as convivial as any in Helsinki. There's a concise snack menu. ⓐ Vilhonkatu 4 ⓣ 010 766 3850 ⓦ www.oluthuone.com ⓛ 13.00–02.00 Mon–Thur, 13.00–03.00 Fri & Sat, 13.00–02.00 Sun ⓜ Tram: 3B, 3T, 4T, 6, 7, 9

CINEMA & ENTERTAINMENT

Kinopalatsi For American mainstream and occasional European films, check the ten screens at this multi-level cinema complex near the railway station. Tickets are discounted for weekday matinées. Cafés, Wi-Fi, shops and game arcades complete the centre. ⓐ Kaisaniemenkatu 2 ⓣ 0600 007 007 ⓦ www.finnkino.fi/kinopalatsi ⓛ From 10.00 daily ⓜ Metro: Kaisaniemi; tram: 3B, 6, 9

Lasipalatsi A multi-purpose entertainment, film and media centre, offering Wi-Fi access, numerous cafés and restaurants, a library, frequent exhibitions and screenings of European films. ⓐ Mannerheimintie 22–24 ⓣ 09 6126 570 ⓦ www.lasipalatsi.fi ⓜ Metro: Rautatientori; tram: 4, 7, 10

Western & northern Helsinki

Broad Mannerheimintie slices the part of Helsinki lying north of Esplanadi neatly in half. Although it may seem as though everything you could want is on the harbour (eastern) side of that line, there is a lot more to see if you cross it. Fewer museums and attractions, perhaps, but more of the city's colourful nightlife and a great deal of its shopping lie in the streets adjoining Uudenmaankatu, Lönnrotinkatu and the shopping street of Fredrikinkatu. Some of the city's most frequently visited attractions are in this area. Among these are not just Temppeliaukio Church (Church in the Rock), the Sibelius Monument and the Olympic Stadium, but also Linnanmäki. This – Finland's biggest amusement park – is its most popular visitor attraction of all.

SIGHTS & ATTRACTIONS

Hietaniemen hautausmaa (Hietaniemi Cemetery)

On All Saints, Christmas and Independence Day, Finns visit cemeteries not only to remember loved ones, but also to honour national heroes and those fallen in wars. Along with the public observations, it's a personal thing with many Finns to remember those who died for their country or who contributed to culture or public life. Hietaniemi is especially busy on 6 December, Independence Day, when the march of students to Senate Square begins here. Buried in its elegant park setting, along with a clutch of presidents in Statesman's Grove, is Marshal Mannerheim, commander-in-chief of Finnish forces in World War II after the Soviet attack on Finland in 1939. Architects Alvar Aalto and Engel and artist Albert Edelfelt rest on Artists' Hill.
ⓐ Mechelininkatu Ⓝ Tram: 8; bus: 15A

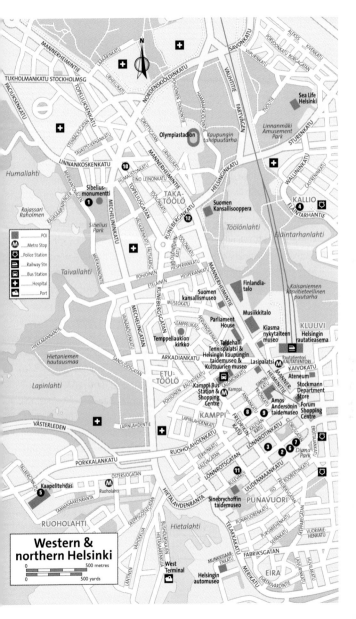

Kaupungin talvipuutarha (Winter Garden)

Near the Olympic Stadium, this vast collection of glasshouses is a tropical paradise perfect for a winter's day. Step inside to stroll beneath towering palms and Norfolk Island pines, and to revel in the passion flowers and camellias that bloom through the winter. Christmas and Easter bring indoor displays of flowers and in the summer the rose gardens are spectacular. ❸ Hammarskjöldintie 1 ❶ 09 3103 9985 ❺ 09.00–15.00 Tues, 12.00–15.00 Wed–Fri, 12.00–16.00 Sat & Sun, closed Mon ❷ Tram: 8

Linnanmäki Amusement Park

From the original 1951 wooden roller coaster to the latest in high-tech thrills, Linnanmäki is fun for all ages. With 44 rides in total, there are 11 specifically for children, 17 suitable for whole families, and 16 major rides which older visitors will enjoy, including a fun house and a hall of mirrors. The park is run by a children's charity foundation and ticket money goes to a good cause. Live shows are performed daily on the outdoor stage, and a free play area, Fairytale Valley, is always popular. ❸ Tivolikuja 1 ❶ 09 773 991 ❾ www.linnanmaki.fi ❺ May–early Sept (hours vary) ❷ Tram: 3B, 9; bus: 23 ❶ Admission charge for rides (entry to area is free)

Olympiastadion (Olympic Stadium)

Built in 1938 by functionalist architects Yrjö Lindegren and Toivo Jäntti for the 1940 Olympics, the stadium was not used because World War II intervened and the Games were cancelled. It was not until the summer of 1952 that the Olympics finally came to the stadium, which is now a venue for athletic and music events. Outside is a statue of runner Paavo Nurmi, 'The Flying Finn', who won the gold medal and carried the Olympic torch the last lap into the stadium for the 1952 Olympiad.

◆ The Olympic Tower is the epitome of 1930s style

The stadium's 72-m (236-ft) tower gives a panoramic view of the city and over the Gulf of Finland, and also at the stadium is the Museum of Finnish Sports. To get there, take the first right from Mannerheimintie after Helsinginkatu or take tram 3T to Nordenskiöldinkatu and walk south on Pohjoinen stadiontie.
ⓐ Paavo Nurmentie 1 ❶ Stadium: 09 4366 010; museum: 09 434 2250 ⓦ Stadium: www.stadion.fi; museum: www.urheilumuseo.org
🕒 Stadium: 09.00–20.00 Mon–Fri, 09.00–18.00 Sat & Sun (closed during events); museum: 11.00–19.00 Mon–Fri, 12.00–16.00 Sat & Sun ⓝ Tram: 3T, 4T, 7, 10 ❶ Admission charge

Sea Life Helsinki

The underwater world of the local Baltic waters, the Arctic and the tropical seas is explored in this series of underwater exhibits. A transparent tunnel takes visitors through these underwater worlds

⬤ *The Sibelius Monument*

inhabited by sea creatures. The environmental impact of human activity is a major theme, dealing with issues such as pollution and the unrestrained harvesting of fish. Aim to be there during feeding times – ask for details at the entrance. ❸ Tivolitie 10 ☎ 09 565 8200 ⓦ www.sealife.fi ⏰ 10.00–17.00 Thur–Tues, 10.00–20.00 Wed (Oct–Apr); 10.00–19.00 daily (May, June, Aug & Sept); 10.00–21.00 daily (July) Ⓝ Tram: 3B, 9 ❶ Admission charge

Sibelius-monumentti (Sibelius Monument)

The great Finnish composer once said that 'Nobody erects a monument to a critic' – and thus expressed a frustration of artists everywhere. He needn't have worried about his own legacy – not only a monument, but an entire Sibelius Park to accommodate it. For the monument, a national competition was held and the winning design was that proposed by Eija Hiltunen. However, its abstract nature was highly controversial and a more conventional effigy of the composer was added alongside. Completed in 1967, ten years after Sibelius' death, the monument consists of over 600 welded steel pipes that make their own music on windy days. Although opinions are still divided, many people love the monument, and the surrounding park is a fine place to stroll or take a picnic. ❸ Sibelius Park, Mechelininkatu 38 ⏰ Daylight hours Ⓝ Bus: 18, 24

Temppeliaukion kirkko (Temppeliaukio Church or Church in the Rock)

Nowhere is the Finns' fascination with architectural experiments more evident than in the Church in the Rock, one of the city's most visited attractions. The notion of carving an entire church out of solid rock is not new, but troglodyte chapels are rarely cut into such a relatively small outcrop in the middle of a city. However, that's exactly what architects Timo and Tuomo Suomalainen did, covering the excavation with a roof of woven copper connected to concrete spokes. The rounded copper roof offsets the deadening effect of the granite walls, creating extraordinary acoustics for concerts, which can range from Christmas chorales to klezmer groups. ❸ Lutherinkatu 3, off Fredrikinkatu ❶ 09 2340 5920 ❷ 10.00–20.00 Mon–Thur, 10.00–17.00 Fri & Sat, 11.45–17.45 Sun (mid-May–mid-Sept); 10.00–17.00 Mon, 10.00–12.45, 14.15–17.00 Tues, 10.00–18.00 Wed & Sat, 10.00–20.00 Thur & Fri, 11.45–13.45, 15.30–18.00 Sun (mid-Sept– mid-May). Hours may vary due to services and concerts ❷ Bus: 18, 24; tram: 3T

CULTURE

Although the area west of Mannerheimintie is better known for its shopping and nightlife than for its cultural attractions, you'll find a great clutch of museums on art and one highlighting Finland's relation to other world cultures.

At the far western edge, Kaapelitehdas (Cable Factory) is a multi-faceted complex of small museums, with a theatre and restaurant.

◗ *The city's most unusual church was hollowed out from granite*

KAAPELITEHDAS (CABLE FACTORY)

The renovated factory overlooking the western docks, a combination of sights under one roof, houses the following trio of small museums and two dance theatre groups, as well as a restaurant. ⓐ Tallberginkatu 1 ❶ 09 4763 8300 ⓦ www.kaapelitehdas.fi Ⓝ Bus/tram: 8, 20, 21, 65A, 66A ❶ Admission charge to museums and performances

Dance Theatre Hurjaruuth This theatre specialises in children's dance performances. ❶ 09 565 7250 ⓦ www.hurjaruuth.fi

Finnish Museum of Photography This museum explores the history and artistry of photography from 1840 to the present. ❶ 09 686 63621 ⓦ www.valokuvataiteenmuseo.fi ❶ 11.00–18.00 Tues–Sun, closed Mon

Hotel and Restaurant Museum Take a look at Finnish food and drink traditions. ❶ 09 6859 3700 ⓦ www.hotellijaravintola museo.fi ❶ 11.00–18.00 Tues–Sun, closed Mon

Theatre Museum This museum offers special exhibits on the history and art of the stage, but its primary focus is on interaction, so visitors can play with the exhibits and try their hand at various forms of theatre art. ❶ 0207 961 670 ⓦ www.teatterimuseo.fi ❶ 11.00–18.00 Tues–Sun, closed Mon

Zodiak Centre for New Dance This centre is a repertory company that explores trends in dance though regular performances. ❶ 09 694 4948 ⓦ www.zodiak.fi

Helsingin kaupungin taidemuseo (Helsinki City Art Museum)

Special exhibitions of Finnish and international art are shown here, often part of an international circuit. Tennispalatsi, Salomonkatu 15 (near the Kamppi shopping centre) 09 310 87001 www.taidemuseo.hel.fi 11.00–20.30 Tues–Sun, closed Mon Metro: Kamppi Admission charge

Kulttuurien museo (Museum of Cultures)

Also housed in Tennispalatsi, this fascinating museum explores the Finnish people (see page 22), as well as telling the story of other cultures through the work of early Finnish explorers and anthropologists. Part of the museum focuses on Chinese artefacts brought to Finland by traders and seafarers in the early 19th century. Salomonkatu 15 09 405 09806 www.nba.fi 11.00–20.00 Tues, 11.00–18.00 Wed–Sun, closed Mon Metro: Kamppi Admission charge

Sinebrychoffin taidemuseo (Sinebrychoff Art Museum)

Finland's finest collection of old masters and other European art from the 1300s to the 1800s is displayed in the furnished mansion of the museum's donors. The rooms, although used as galleries, have fine parquet floors and other interior features. Miniatures and porcelain collections are especially impressive. Bulevardi 40 09 1733 6460 www.sinebrychoffintaidemuseo.fi 10.00–18.00 Tues & Fri, 10.00–20.00 Wed & Thur, 11.00–17.00 Sat & Sun, closed Mon Tram: 6 Admission charge

Taidehalli (Kunsthalle)

Changing exhibitions of contemporary art highlight young artists as well as those who have already established a reputation. Taidehallin

Klubi, the gallery's restaurant, is open for lunch and evening meals Monday–Saturday and the bar is open Monday–Saturday until 02.00. Nervanderinkatu 3 040 450 7211 www.taidehalli.fi 11.00–18.00 Tues, Thur & Fri, 11.00–20.00 Wed, 11.00–17.00 Sat & Sun, closed Mon Bus: 24; metro: Kamppi Admission charge

RETAIL THERAPY

The lovely Fredrikinkatu and its adjoining streets are known for their fashion and interior-décor boutiques. Stroll Bulevardi to browse or buy art and antiques. Forum is the biggest shopping complex in the city centre, facing on to Mannerheimintie and filling the entire area between it and Yrjönkatu. Kamppi Shopping Centre has a variety of designer shops, restaurants and cafés, and is conveniently located above the main bus station (see page 51).

Aero Find a piece of vintage Alvar Aalto, or the work of other Finnish designers in this shop that specialises in 1930–70 Finnish design and furnishings. Yrjönkatu 8 09 680 2185 www.aerodesignfurniture.fi 10.00–18.00 Mon–Fri, 11.00–15.00 Sat, closed Sun Tram: 3B, 6, 9, 10

Antiq Bulevard It won't be cheap, but it will be good if you find it in this high-class antiquerie. Hours are eccentric, so call or just stop in if it's open. Vuorimiehenkatu 10 040 552 1764 Tram: 1A, 3B; bus: 16

Bisarri Here you'll find modern Finnish design alongside glassware, ceramics, textiles and gorgeous utility items. Hietalahti Market Hall, Hietalahdentori 0500 872 922 www.bisarri.fi 10.00–17.00 Mon–Fri, 10.00–15.00 Sat, closed Sun Tram: 6

Galerie 1900 *Jugendstil*'s back in vogue and, of course, Helsinki's the place to find it. The shop offers lighting fixtures and décor items in *Jugendstil* and Art Deco style. Annankatu 11 09 649 152 Hours vary; call before visiting Tram: 10

Globe Hope Feel stylish *and* virtuous: this innovative Finnish company creates a range of products from recycled materials, including clothes, shoes, bags and household items such as aprons. Mannerheimintie 22–24 (rear of Lasipalatsi) 050 530 2103 www.globehope.com 10.00–20.00 Mon–Fri, 10.00–18.00 Sat, closed Sun Metro: Rautatientori; tram: 3B, 3T, 4, 4T, 7A, 7B, 10

Helsinki 10 Trendy shop of vintage designer clothes, music and art books. Eerikinkatu 3 050 559 6504 www.helsinki10.com 11.00–19.00 Mon–Fri, 10.00–18.00 Sat, closed Sun Tram: 3B, 3T, 6, 9, 10

Hietalahti Flea Market Be prepared to bargain for everything from cut-price clothes to antiques. The latter may include the family treasures of someone settling an estate or just having a clear-out, as well as regular dealers. Hietalahdentori 08.00–19.00 Mon–Fri, 08.00–16.00 Sat, 10.00–16.00 Sun (May–Sept); 09.00–17.00 Mon–Fri, 08.00–16.00 Sat, closed Sun (Oct–Apr) Tram: 6

Hietalahti Market Hall Architect Selim Lindqvist's historic building, across the square from the flea market, is filled with shops and stalls selling local handicrafts, plus cafés. Hietalahdentori 10.00–17.00 Mon–Fri, 10.00–15.00 Sat, closed Sun Tram: 6

Ivana Helsinki Campus Visionary stylish clothes for an easy lifestyle, Ivana's threads are rich in outdoor themes and designed to be lived in.

ⓐ Uudenmaankatu 15 ⓣ 09 622 4422 ⓦ www.ivanahelsinki.com
ⓛ 11.00–19.00 Mon–Fri, 11.00–16.00 Sat, closed Sun ⓝ Tram: 3B, 6

Limbo Shop Limbo's easy styles flow with the season, from comfortable sundresses in cheery colours to jumpers and T-shirts with a sense of humour. Hip clothes don't get more comfortable.
ⓐ Annankatu 13 ⓣ 09 644 060 ⓦ www.limbo.fi ⓛ 11.00–18.00 Mon–Fri, 11.00–16.00 Sat, closed Sun ⓝ Tram: 3B, 6, 9

Miun If you like Finnish designer clothing, jewellery, accessories and ceramic statues, you should make this your first stop.
ⓐ Uudenmaankatu 14 ⓣ 050 352 8893 ⓦ www.miun.fi ⓛ 11.00–18.00 Mon–Fri, 11.00–16.00 Sat, closed Sun ⓝ Tram: 3B, 6, 9

Myymälä2 A no-frills environment where young artists can show their work, Myymälä2 has launched several talents, as well as creating a venue for gallery-goers. The boutique is a gold mine of groovy gifts and funky finds. ⓐ Uudenmaankatu 23 ⓦ www.myymala2.com ⓛ 12.00–18.00 Wed–Sat, 12.00–17.00 Sun, closed Mon & Tues ⓝ Tram: 3B, 6

Nemaki A swish boutique offering luxury clothes by Scandinavian designer Irja Leimu. ⓐ Tarkk'ampujankatu 20 ⓣ 09 631 353
ⓛ 13.00–17.00 Tues–Fri, 12.00–14.00 Sat, closed Sun & Mon
ⓦ www.nemaki.fi ⓝ Tram: 3B

Popparienkeli Whatever you need in new or used vinyl from the 1950s and 60s or CDs from the 80s onwards, you're likely to find it here. But ask, since not everything is displayed. Look for other music shops in this vicinity. ⓐ Fredrikinkatu 12 ⓣ 09 661 638 ⓦ www.popangel.fi
ⓛ 10.00–18.00 Mon–Fri, 10.00–16.00 Sat, closed Sun ⓝ Tram: 3B, 3T

Punavuoren Peikko The coolest shop in Helsinki for children's clothes and toys, many by Scandinavian designers. ⓐ Uudenmaankatu 15 ❶ 045 120 0823 ⓦ www.punavuorenpeikko.fi ❷ 10.30–18.00 Mon–Fri, 10.30–16.00 Sat, closed Sun Ⓝ Tram: 3B, 6, 9, 10

Le Slip Shop for undergarments at uberprices, all from the best designers. ⓐ Annankatu 6 ❶ 09 640 762 ❷ 11.00–18.00 Mon–Fri, 11.00–15.00 Sat, closed Sun Ⓝ Tram: 3B

Stupido Shop If it's on DVD, tape, CD or vinyl, and it's alternative, from *humppa* to the latest Aavikko, just ask the Stupido guys. ⓐ Iso Roobertinkatu 23 ❶ 09 646 990 ⓦ www.stupido.fi ❷ 09.00–20.00 Mon–Fri, 10.00–18.00 Sat, closed Sun ❶ 09 646 990 Ⓝ Tram: 3B

TAKING A BREAK

The mega-malls Forum and Kamppi both have a number of cafés and small eating places. It's a good rule that wherever shoppers congregate, there will be places to stop for coffee and compare finds.

Café Regatta £ ❶ Cosy, quirky little waterside café in a former fishermen's shed a stone's throw from the Sibelius Monument; also has a more spacious terrace. Warm up with a traditional Finnish pastry on those chillier days. ⓐ Merikannontie 10 ❶ 0400 760 049 ❷ 10.00–23.00 daily Ⓝ Bus: 18, 24 ❶ Cash only

Café Bar No 9 ££ ❷ Cool and trendy place to eat during the day. Good for drinks in the evening as well. ⓐ Uudenmaankatu 9 ❶ 09 621 4059 ⓦ www.bar9.net ❷ 11.00–02.00 Mon–Fri, 12.00–02.00 Sat & Sun Ⓝ Tram: 3B, 6, 9, 10

Café Ekberg ££ ❸ Helsinki's oldest café, Ekberg isn't just a period piece, it's a bit of romantic old Europe. Reminiscent of between-the-wars Vienna, it's the kind of place you expect to see writers working on their books. They serve a breakfast buffet, lunch, light meals and tasty pastries or a glass of something in between. ❸ Bulevardi 9 ❶ 09 6811 8660 Ⓦ www.cafeekberg.fi Ⓛ 07.30–19.00 Mon–Fri, 08.30–17.00 Sat, 09.00–17.00 Sun Ⓝ Tram: 3B, 6

Café Piritta ££ ❹ Smart new café on the shore of Eläintarhanlahti, with the added novelty (in summer) of its own water-bus service from Kauppatori (approximately hourly). The lunchtime buffet is good value. ❸ Eläintarhantie 12 ❶ 09 753 1732 Ⓦ http://ursula. fi/piritta Ⓛ 09.00–22.00 Sun–Tues, 09.00–24.00 Wed–Sat Ⓝ Metro: Hakaniemi; tram: 1, 1A, 3B, 3T

⬤ *Café Regatta has a great location close to the Sibelius Monument*

Hima & Sali ££ ❺ If you've made the trek out to Kaapelitehdas, this is a great spot to relax and sample the special coffee, freshly baked pastries and great bread. There's an ever-changing art display and free Wi-Fi, too. ⓐ Tallberginkatu 1C ❶ 09 694 1701 Ⓦ www.himasali.com ❷ 08.30–21.00 Mon–Fri (lunch 11.00–14.30), 12.00–19.00 Sat & Sun Ⓝ Metro: Ruoholahti; tram: 8

AFTER DARK

Along with having some of the hottest clubs and entertainment venues in the city, the neighbourhoods away from Esplanadi are also the 'low rent district' for bars and pubs. Iso Roobertinkatu is known for its restaurants, pubs and bars, which fill almost the entire street. While a number of places have age limits that cut out those below 20 or 24, most of those around the Kamppi metro station do not, so, traditionally, this is where the under-20s hang out.

RESTAURANTS

Rafla ££ ❻ Modern European cuisine with a touch of French and Scandinavian home cooking. Excellent espresso, good wines and a nice atmosphere. ⓐ Uudenmaankatu 9 ❶ 09 6124 2244 Ⓦ www.ravintolarafla.fi ❷ 11.00–02.00 Mon–Fri, 13.00–02.00 Sat (kitchen closes 23.00), closed Sun Ⓝ Tram: 3B, 6, 9

Demo ££–£££ ❼ Offering high-class home-made food combined with personal and friendly service, Demo was recently awarded a much-coveted Michelin star. ⓐ Uudenmaankatu 9–11 ❶ 09 2289 0840 Ⓦ www.restaurantdemo.fi ❷ 16.00–23.00 Tues–Sat, closed Sun & Mon Ⓝ Tram: 3B, 6, 9, 10

Helmi ££–£££ The stylish décor sets the tone for equally well-designed dishes. The inspiration is global and eclectic, and the vegetarian fare is as well planned and original as the other choices – try honey-and-soy-glazed fennel, for example. Even the plain-sounding dish of chicken and vegetables is a winner. Minimum age is 24. ⓐ Eerikinkatu 14 ⓣ 09 612 6410 ⓦ www. ravintolahelmi.fi ⓛ 17.00–24.00 Tues–Thur, 17.00–04.00 Fri & Sat, closed Sun & Mon ⓝ Metro: Kamppi

Kosmos ££–£££ ⓿ A Helsinki institution since 1924, serving delicious classic dishes from duck and chateaubriand to champagne sorbet and pancakes. ⓐ Kalevankatu 3 ⓣ 09 647 255 ⓦ www.ravintolakosmos.fi ⓛ 11.30–01.00 Mon–Fri, 16.00–01.00 Sat, closed Sun ⓝ Metro: Kamppi

Lehtovaara ££–£££ ⓾ The menu speaks for itself at this exceptional restaurant near the Sibelius Park: fillet of beef with deep-fried garlic potatoes, garlic butter and fried fresh mushroom slices, lightly smoked Arctic char with lobster ravioli or snowgrouse breast with a cake of root vegetables and potato. Vegetarians might be offered cheese polenta with ginger-braised vegetables. ⓐ Mechelininkatu 39 ⓣ 09 440 833 ⓦ www.lehtovaararavintola.fi ⓛ 11.00–24.00 Mon–Fri (16.00–22.00 in July), 16.00–24.00 Sat, 13.00–21.00 Sun ⓝ Bus: 18, 24, 42

Saaga ££–£££ ⓫ The sights, sounds and of course the flavours of Lapland are the all-encompassing theme at Saaga; in other hands this could be tacky, but here it's done with total conviction. Needless to say, the menu is heavy on reindeer, but you could also try bear soup followed by glow-fried arctic char. ⓐ Bulevardi 34

℡ 09 7425 5544 **Ⓦ** www.asrestaurants.com **Ⓛ** 18.00–23.00 Mon–Sat, closed Sun (mid-Aug–mid-June) **Ⓝ** Tram: 6

Ravintola Carelia & Winebar £££ ⑫ The wine list alone is staggering, with over 300 varieties, including 50 different champagnes, making it a good place to stop before or after the opera, just across the street. Menu choices are just as difficult. Begin maybe with cep soup with thyme foam, then go on to guineafowl breast with truffle risotto and bacon. **Ⓐ** Mannerheimintie 56 **℡** 09 2709 0976 **Ⓦ** www.carelia.info **Ⓛ** 11.00–24.00 Mon–Fri, 16.00–24.00 Sat, closed Sun **Ⓝ** Tram: 3T, 4, 7, 10

BARS & CLUBS

Cuba As well as the best *mojitos* in town, this place has DJs and wild late-night parties. **Ⓐ** Erottajankatu 4 **℡** 050 325 9522 **Ⓦ** www.cubacafe.fi **Ⓛ** 17.00–24.00 Tues, 17.00–02.00 Wed & Thur, 17.00–04.00 Fri & Sat, closed Sun **Ⓝ** Tram: 10

Dante's Highlight Back in 1878 this building was a church; now it's a raucous three-storey nightclub with several dance floors, a wide range of music and a young clientele – it's one of the few clubs that admit 18-year-olds. **Ⓐ** Fredrikinkatu 42 **℡** 010 766 3780 **Ⓦ** www.danteshighlight.fi **Ⓛ** 12.00–04.00 Mon–Fri, 16.00–04.00 Sat & Sun **Ⓝ** Metro: Kamppi **❶** Admission charge (free 22.00–23.00)

DTM No one has disputed DTM's claim to be the biggest combo of gay café, bar, disco and nightclub in the Nordic countries. Taking it from the top, the upstairs has a cruise ship-style dance floor with a disco and traditional dance music on Friday and Saturday. The street level is a café, with Internet access. Downstairs, the nightclub has live music, dance and shows, with a killer sound system and over-the-top lighting and video tech. Special nights offer top drag shows, bubbling foam parties and more. Minimum age 18 between 18.00 and 21.00; after 21.00 it's 24 (those younger will be ejected). Iso Roobertinkatu 28 010 841 6969 www.dtm.fi 10.00–04.00 Mon–Sat, 13.00–04.00 Sun Tram: 3B Admission charge on Saturday nights and for special events

Lost and Found Gay, straight, whatever. Everyone is welcome and feels at home in this modern restaurant/club/bar/disco. Call it Lostari, to feel like a local. Best to go early, since queues form on the big party nights – Wednesday, Friday, Saturday – before midnight. Annankatu 6 09 680 1010 www.lostandfound.fi 20.00–04.00 daily Tram: 3B Age 24 and over

O'Malley's A Finnish take on an Irish pub, but a good stop for a pint if you're over 20. Sokos Hotel, Yrjönkatu 26 020 1234 604 16.00–01.00 Mon–Thur, 14.00–02.00 Fri & Sat, closed Sun Tram: 3T

Royal Onnela Big disco, table-dancing and a section for metal, this place is especially popular because the €5 membership card buys you beers for €1 from 23.00 to 01.00 most nights. Fredrikinkatu 48 020 775 9460 www.onnelahelsinki.fi 21.00–04.00 Wed–Sat, closed Sun–Tues Metro: Kamppi

St Urho's Pub Turn right as you leave the National Museum and you'll find this busy pub right next to Storyville (below). It has a great selection of beers, and a well-priced menu of honest pub grub and pizzas. Museokatu 10 09 5807 7222 www.botta.fi 15.00–01.00 Sun–Tues, 15.00–03.00 Wed–Sat Tram: 4, 7, 10

Storyville The city's premier jazz club, Storyville offers live jazz in an environment that favours listening to the New Orleans-style music and enjoying a drink. The pub upstairs provides a place to wait for the crowd to thin on weekends. There is a terrace outside for fine evenings and daytime drinks. ⓐ Museokatu 8 ⓣ 09 408 007 ⓦ www.storyville.fi ⓛ 20.00–04.00 Wed–Sat, closed Sun–Tues ⓝ Tram: 4, 7, 10. ⓘ Admission charge (summer terrace is free)

Tavastia You can witness the country's major bands in action at Finland's leading rock venue. ⓐ Urho Kekkosen katu 4–6 ⓣ 09 774 67420 ⓦ www.tavastiaklubi.fi ⓛ 20.00–01.00 Sun–Thur, 20.00–04.00 Fri & Sat ⓝ Metro: Kamppi

The Tiger The classiest club in town is on two floors on top of the Kamppi shopping centre. Large dance floors and top-quality sound systems – what more could you want? ⓐ Urho Kekkosen katu 1 ⓣ 020 775 9350 ⓦ www.thetiger.fi ⓛ 22.00–04.00 Wed–Sat, closed Sun–Tues ⓝ Metro: Kamppi

ENTERTAINMENT

Tennispalatsi The indoor tennis stadium was built in 1938 for the Olympics that never happened (see page 88), but the Finns have put it to good use as a sports area and entertainment venue. Among other things, it contains the Helsinki City Art Museum and Museum of Cultures (see page 95), a **14-screen cinema** (ⓣ 0600 007 007 ⓦ www.finnkino.fi ⓛ Box office from 10.00 daily) and numerous cafés and restaurants. Nearby is the Kamppi shopping centre (see page 96) and bus station. It's a great place to visit on a rainy day or if you have kids in tow, as there's plenty to keep you occupied all day. ⓐ Salomonkatu 15 ⓝ Metro: Kamppi

The islands & outskirts

Helsinki sits in the midst of an archipelago and some of its most outstanding attractions are on the islands. Chief among them is the UNESCO World Heritage Site of Suomenlinna Fortress, which consists of a small cluster of islands interconnected by bridges and sandbars. On Suomenlinna you'll find enough museums, craft studios and restaurants to keep you occupied all day. Animal lovers will enjoy the zoo on Korkeasaari, where rare animals have plenty of room to roam. Those hankering after some time on the beach can head to Pihlajasaari or Uunisaari islands. As well as dedicated excursion boats which tour the archipelago, there are frequent ferries to Suomenlinna throughout the year and to the other main islands in the summer months. Ferry trips provide an inexpensive way of getting afloat and are included in the Helsinki Card (see page 58).

SIGHTS & ATTRACTIONS

Boat trips

You can enjoy the views of elegant Helsinki and get a cheap mini-cruise by taking the ferry between Kauppatori (Market Square) and Suomenlinna Fortress. Boats for Suomenlinna leave less frequently from Katajanokka, east of Market Square. For timetables see ⓦ www.hkl.fi or ask at the tourist office.

In the summer months, ferries also travel from Market Square to Korkeasaari, where the zoo is located, and continue on to Hakaniemenranta quay in the Kallio neighbourhood north of the railway station, where there is also a daily market. Another ferry leaves from the southern tip of the city (in the Eira neighbourhood), bound for Pihlajasaari, a beach-ringed island west of Suomenlinna.

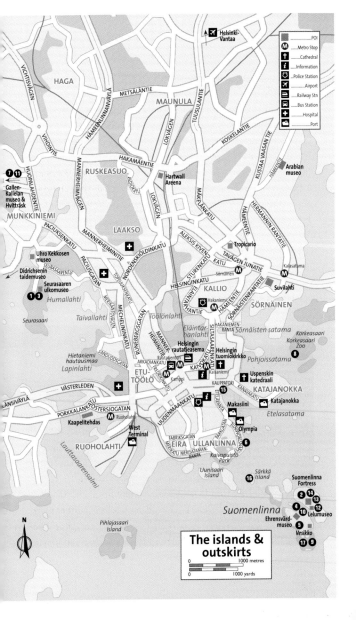

POI
Ⓜ Metro Stop
✝ Cathedral
ℹ Information
Police Station
✈ Airport
Railway Stn
Bus Station
✚ Hospital
Port

Helsinki-Vantaa ✈

HAGA

MAUNULA

MÄTSÄLÄNTIE

VIHTISVÄGEN

METSÄLÄNTIE

HÄMEENLINNANVÄYLÄ

LOKVÄGEN

TUUSULANTIE

KOSKELANTIE

HUOPALAHDENTIE

Gallen-Kallelan museo & Hvitträsk ❼ ⓫

RUSKEASUO

HAKAMÄENTIE

Hartwall Arena

MANNERHEIMVÄGEN

ADOLGATAN

LOKVÄGEN

MÄKELANKATU

KUSTAA VAASAN TIE

HÄMEENTIE

HERMANNIN RANTATIE

Arabian museo

MUNKKINIEMI

PACIUKSENKATU

LAAKSO

MANNERHEIMINTIE

NORDENSKÖLDINKATU

ALEKSIS KIVEN KATU

STUREN KATU

TAVÄGEN JUNATIE

Tropicario

HELSINGINKATU

Kalasatama

Uhro Kekkonen museo

Didrichsenin taidemuseo

Seurasaaren ulkomuseo ❶ ❸

PACIUKSENKATU

SEURASARENTIE

TÖÖLÖNKATU

MECHELINKATU

Humalahti

HÄMEENTIE

LÄNTINEN

Sörnäinen Ⓜ

KALLIO

Suvilahti

SÖRNÄISTENRANTATIE

SÖRNÄINEN

Seurasaari

Taivallahti

Töölönlahti

Hakaniemi Ⓜ

HÄMEENTIE

Hietaniemi hautausmaa

Lapinlahti

RUNEBERGSGATAN

MANNERHEIMINTIE

MECHELININKATU

SANDUDDSGATAN

Eläintarhanlahti

SILTASAARENKATU

HÄKANIEMEN-RANTA

Sörnäisten satama

Korkeasaari

Korkeasaari Zoo ❽

Helsingin rautatieasema

Rautatientori

Helsingin tuomiokirkko ✝

Pohjoissatama

VÄSTERLEDEN

ETU-TÖÖLÖ

ARKADIANKATU

FREDRIKINKATU

Kamppi

KANAVKATU

Kaisaniemi

ℹ

Uspenskin katedraali ✝

LÄNSIVÄYLA

PORKKALANKATU ÖSTERSJOGATAN

Ruoholahti Ⓜ

UUDENMAANKATU

ℹ ⓯

KAUPPATORI

Makasiini

KANAVAKATU

KATAJANOKKA

Katajanokka

Etelasatama

Kaapelitehdas

West Terminal

FABRIKSGATAN

EIRA

MERIKATU MERISATAMAN-RANTA

ULLANLINNA

BULEVARDI

Olympia

❻

RUOHOLAHTI

Lauttasaarensalmi

Kaivopuisto Park

Uunisaari Island

Särkkä Island

Suomenlinna Fortress

❹ ❷ ⓬

❿ ⓱ Lelumuseo

Ehrensvärd-museo

❺ Vesikko

⓰ Island

❶❼ ❾

Pihlajasaari Island

Suomenlinna

N

The islands & outskirts

0 ————— 1000 metres
0 ————— 1000 yards

As boat timetables vary according to season and weather, it's best to consult the tourist office on arrival (see page 153).

A number of traditional cruise boats ply the waters around Helsinki between May and September. **Sun Lines** (☎ 020 741 8210 ⓦ www.sunlines.fi) explores the tree-lined Degerö Canal, Korkeasaari Zoo, the Finnish icebreakers and the cruise-ship harbours, along with circling Suomenlinna Fortress, in comfortable cruisers that offer a coffee and drinks bar. **IHA Lines** (☎ 09 6874 5050 ⓦ www.ihalines.fi) offers à la carte dining on their boats as they cruise through the archipelago on trips that last from 90 minutes to three hours. Three different routes, each beginning at Market Square, cover the eastern islands or the fortress and surrounding islands. Booking is essential for dining cruises. Along with archipelago cruises, **Royal Line** (☎ 0207 118 333 ⓦ www.royalline.fi) offers daily trips to the medieval town of Porvoo in July and August (see page 124).

Korkeasaaren eläintarha (Korkeasaari Zoo)

More than just a place for visitors to view exotic wildlife, Helsinki's zoo is a well-respected leader in the preservation and breeding of endangered species. Their snow leopard successes are legendary in zoo annals, and they continue to house rare species of big cats. Currently these include, in addition to snow leopards, the Siberian tiger, of which there are only a few hundred remaining, and the exceedingly rare Asian lion from India. Rare Arctic species include the polar fox and musk ox, whose hair is a metre (3ft) long to protect it from icy winters. Environments represented range from tropical rainforests to arctic tundra, and the collections include 200 species of animals, with 1,000 species of plants to make them feel at home. Founded in 1889, it is one of the oldest zoos in the

● *Escape from the city to the tranquillity of the forested islands*

world. ⓐ Korkeasaari ⓣ 0600 95 911 (24 hr info) or 09 310 1615 (switchboard) ⓦ www.korkeasaari.fi ⓛ 10.00–20.00 daily (May–Aug); 10.00–18.00 daily (Apr & Sept); 10.00–16.00 daily (Oct–Mar) ⓝ Bus: 11; ferry from Market Square or Hakaniemi (May–Sept) ⓘ Admission charge

Pihlajasaari Island
To get away from it all and luxuriate in the sun on an island in the Gulf of Finland, take the boat to the rocks and beaches of Pihlajasaari. Rent a private changing cabin or bare it all on the nudist beach. (You will, however, need clothes for the café and the boat ride!) ⓣ 09 534 806 ⓦ www.jt-line.fi ⓛ mid-May–early Sept ⓝ Boats depart from Merisatamanranta

Suomenlinna Fortress
One of the world's largest sea fortresses, the 18th-century fort on Suomenlinna has a fascinating past and an interesting present. A 15-minute ferry ride from Market Square brings you to the group of connected islands, where there is enough to do to occupy an entire day – and in the summer, an evening, too. It was built in 1747 by the Swedes, who owned Finland then, to scare off the Russians, who eventually captured both it and Finland, turning the island's guns figuratively to the west. The impressive fortifications became a UNESCO World Heritage Site in 1991.

In the visitor centre a wide-screen show, *The Suomenlinna Experience*, explores the fortress's long history, in English. Sign up here for guided walks that help bring all the sites into a unified picture. In the same building is the museum, which shows how soldiers lived during the Swedish and Russian rules. Suomenlinna was also used by the Finns after independence as a prison, a garrison, a submarine base and as a base for the Valmet shipyard, which made ships as reparations to the Soviet Union after World War II.

Walking and cycling paths (you must bring bicycles from the mainland as none are hired out here) lead along the cliffs and to small beaches. Be careful on the cliff paths, since these are not fenced, and when on the beaches with children, because of dangerous sudden ship wakes and currents. Various buildings house studios and shops of glassblowers, potters and other craftsmen. ❶ 09 684 1880 Ⓦ www.suomenlinna.fi ❹ Visitor centre: 10.00–18.00 daily (May–Sept); 10.30–16.30 daily (Oct–Apr) Ⓝ Ferry from Market Square (daily) or Katajanokka (Mon–Fri); visit Ⓦ www.hkl.fi for timetables

Uunisaari Island

Just off the southern tip of the city and reached by boat from Kompassitori near Kaivopuisto Park (mid-Apr–mid-Nov) or via a pontoon bridge (mid-Nov–mid-Apr), Uunisaari offers sand beaches with lifeguards, a café, a restaurant and a sauna. The well-protected beach is safe for children. ❶ 09 636 870 Ⓦ www.uunisaari.com

CULTURE

Arabian museo (Arabia Museum)

The Arabia company began in 1874, and moved into the design of modern tableware in the 1930s. But it was not until the 1960s that it became a worldwide name in smart dinnerware and porcelain design. Follow the history of this well-known company, along with the development of Finnish and modern design in home furnishings in the museum, where 1,600 examples of utility and decorative porcelain from the past 125 years are shown. You'll also find the company's factory outlet shop here (see page 115), with excellent

bargains on imperfect and overstocked items. ⓐ Hämeentie 135
ⓣ 0204 3910 ⓦ www.arabiamuseum.fi ⓛ 12.00–18.00 Tues–Fri,
10.00–16.00 Sat & Sun, closed Mon ⓝ Tram: 6, 8 ⓘ Admission charge

Didrichsenin taidemuseo (Didrichsen Art Museum)

A couple's private collection is now a museum rich in 20th-century
art, along with specialised collections of Asian antiquities and pre-
Columbian art. Primary here is the Finnish art from the 20th century,
including works by Edelfelt and his contemporaries. Non-Finnish modern
art includes works by Picasso, Kandinsky and Miró. ⓐ Kuusilahdenkuja 1,
Kuusisaari ⓣ 09 477 8330 ⓦ www.didrichsenmuseum.fi ⓛ 11.00–17.00
Tues–Sun, closed Mon ⓝ Bus: 194, 195 from Elielinaukio, bay 36
(near the post office), 503, 506 ⓘ Admission charge

Gallen-Kallelan museo (Gallen-Kallela Museum)

The most important Finnish artist of the early 1900s, Gallen-Kallela
had a rich and varied career in painting, drawing, graphics, sculpture,
posters, photographs and applied art, all of which are represented in
this museum. It also tells about the artist's colourful life and times.
Gallen-Kallela designed this *Jugendstil* home and studio, built
1911–1913. The wooden Tarvaspää villa, built in the 1850s, houses a café.
ⓐ Gallen-Kallelantie 27, Espoo ⓣ 09 849 2340 ⓦ www.gallen-kallela.fi
ⓛ 11.00–18.00 daily (mid-May–Aug); 11.00–16.00 Tues–Sat, 11.00–17.00
Sun, closed Mon (Sept–mid-May) ⓝ Tram: 4 to Munkkiniemi, alight at
Laajalahdenaukio, then walk through Munkinpuisto Park; shuttle bus
from Munkkiniemen puistotie Mon–Fri only ⓘ Admission charge

Hvitträsk

If the artistic buzz of the Arts and Crafts/*Jugendstil* period fires your
imagination, it's worth the 30-km (18-mile) bus ride to visit the local

MUSEUMS ON SUOMENLINNA

At least half a dozen museums are open during the summer on Suomenlinna. The pick of the bunch are: the **Ehrensvärd-museo** (Ehrensvärd Museum ☎ 09 684 1850 ⏱ 11.00–18.00 daily (June–Aug); 11.00–16.00 daily (May & Sept)), in the former home of the fort's designer and commander Augustin Ehrensvärd, which depicts the earliest Swedish period with models, arms, furniture and paintings; the **Lelumuseo** (Doll and Toy Museum ☎ 040 500 6607 ⓦ www.lelumuseo.fi ⏱ 10.00–18.00 daily (June–Aug); 10.00–17.00 daily (Apr, May & Sept); open some weekends in winter), displaying dolls, doll's houses, teddy bears and other toys from the 1830s to the present in an old Russian villa which is well worth seeing in its own right; and lastly, the 250-ton submarine *Vesikko* (☎ 0299 530 260 ⏱ 11.00–18.00 daily (mid-May–Aug)), which was originally commissioned by the German Navy but actually used by the Finnish Navy from 1936 until the end of World War II. ⓐ Suomenlinna ⓦ www.vesikko.fi

shrine to this style, built as home and studio to some of its most illustrious exponents. Designed by architects Herman Gesellius, Armas Lindgren and Eliel Saarinen, the log-and-stone home is the epitome of the National Romantic style. The architects all lived and worked there at some point, and it was here that the plans were drawn for the Helsinki Railway Station among others of the firm's most famous works. This was the boyhood home of Eliel's son, Eero Saarinen, known for designing American buildings and monuments such as the Gateway Arch in St Louis, Missouri. ⓐ Hvitträskintie 166,

Luoma ☎ 09 4050 9630 ⓦ www.nba.fi 🕐 11.00–17.00 daily
(May–Sept); 11.00–17.00 Wed–Sun, closed Mon & Tues (Oct–Apr)
🚍 Bus: 165 from Kamppi (bay 55) to Hvitträskintie; train: L or U to
Luoma ❶ Admission charge

Seurasaaren ulkomuseo (Seurasaari Open-Air Museum)

Historic buildings from all over Finland have been moved to this
outdoor museum, beautifully insulated from modern-day Helsinki
on its own island. The village of 87 buildings centres around the
farmstead, a working farm where livestock and crops are raised using
old methods. Grander by far is the 18th-century Kahiluoto manor
house, while the oldest building preserved here is the wooden
Karuna church from the 1600s. A regular series of workshops and
programmes highlight folk life and traditional skills for visitors.
ⓐ Seurasaari ☎ 09 4050 9660 ⓦ www.nba.fi 🕐 11.00–17.00
daily (June–Aug); 09.00–15.00 Mon–Fri, 11.00–17.00 Sat & Sun
(late May & early Sept) 🚍 Bus: 24 ❶ Admission charge

Summer Theatre

During summer, you have the chance to see traditional Finnish
perfomances on Suomenlinna and Seurasaari islands. Productions
are in Finnish but, apart from the occasional play, language is not
a barrier to enjoyment since the programme is generally based
on movement, action, dance and music. For tickets, contact
Lippupalvelu (see page 22) or the Stockmann or Sokos department
stores (see pages 79 & 80).

Urho Kekkosen museo (Kekkonen Museum)

The former home of Finland's most famous president, Urho
Kekkonen, is a fine villa set in a park estate adjacent to the island of

Seurasaari. Tamminiemi Villa was his official residence during his presidency, from 1956 to 1981. The villa is furnished with outstanding examples of Finnish design and art, as well as gifts of state. In the summer, the tour includes the sauna, which was the scene of a number of high-level meetings between Soviet and Western diplomats during the Cold War. ⓐ Seurasaarentie 15 ⓘ 09 4050 9650 ⓦ www.nba.fi ⓝ Bus: 24 ⓘ Admission charge. The museum is undergoing renovations until 2012: check opening times via website or by phone

RETAIL THERAPY

Outside the busy and trendy shopping streets of downtown Helsinki, the islands and outer suburbs nonetheless offer some quality shopping. Suomenlinna Fortress houses a number of excellent artisan studios, and museum shops offer unique speciality gifts. And Arabia's factory outlet is a mecca for bargain hunters with a taste for fine dinnerware.

Arabia Factory Shop One of the Nordic countries' best-known brands of porcelain and dinnerware, Arabia spans all ages and tastes with its classic lines and functional style. The outlet offers discontinued styles and seconds at deep discounts. Along with the Arabia label are goods in Iittala and other company brands. See page 112 for address and contact details. ⓘ 10.00–20.00 Mon–Fri, 10.00–16.00 Sat & Sun

Arts and Crafts Summer Shop Selected traditional and modern crafts in all media. ⓐ Building B 34, Suomenlinna ⓘ 050 408 2902 ⓘ 10.00–17.00 daily (mid-May–Sept)

Bastion Hårleman, Susisaari Artisans' studios, some of which are open to the public in the summer. You can call ahead to check, but it's easiest just to wander down on a sunny day and browse.
ⓐ Building B 31, Suomenlinna ⓣ 040 533 7903

Hvitträsk Museum Shop A source of the beautiful Kalevala and Kaunis *koru* jewellery, based on designs from Finnish folklore, this outstanding shop also carries art and architecture books and prints,

🔺 *Sagamaa hand-made glassware is widely available*

and crafts made by the Friends of Finnish Handicrafts. The local artwork includes glass art, jewellery, ceramics, sculpture, woollens and linen tablecloths. ⓐ Hvittäskintie 166, Luoma ❶ 09 4050 9630 ⓦ www.nba.fi ❹ 11.00–17.00 daily (May–Sept); 11.00–17.00 Wed–Sun, closed Mon & Tues (Oct–Apr) ❷ Trains: L and U to Luoma

Hytti ry This studio is a place where one can worship at the altar of the glass-blower's art. Phone to check opening times. ⓐ Building B 48, Suomenlinna ❶ 09 668 727

Jetty Barracks Gallery Operated by the Helsinki Artists' Association, this gallery puts on exhibitions of varied contemporary art in the rooms of the Jetty Barracks. ⓐ Iso Mustasaari, next to the Main Quay, Suomenlinna ❶ 09 673 140 ⓦ www.suomenlinna.fi ❹ 12.00–17.30 Tues–Thur, 11.30–16.00 Fri–Sun, closed Mon

Pot Viapori Ceramics Studio ⓐ Building B 45, Suomenlinna ❶ 09 668 151 ⓦ www.viapori.fi ❹ 12.00–17.00 daily (mid-July–late Aug)

Safari Shop Korkeasaari Zoo's own brand of animal-themed and environmentally friendly products, as well as Fairtrade products and crafts from cooperatives in developing countries, are sold in the zoo shop. ⓐ Korkeasaari ❶ 09 696 2370 ❹ 10.00–20.00 daily (May–Aug); 10.00–18.00 daily (Apr & Sept); 10.00–16.00 daily (Oct–Mar)

Seurasaari Museum Shop Traditional Finnish handicrafts, authentic sauna products, books and other historical items are available in the museum store. ⓐ Seurasaari ❶ 09 4050 9662 ❹ 11.00–17.00 daily (June–Aug); 09.00–15.00 Mon–Fri, 11.00–17.00 Sat & Sun (late May & early Sept)

TAKING A BREAK

Nearly every museum has its own café, usually open for the same hours as the museum itself. Suomenlinna is well supplied with eating places, several of which are listed on page 120, since they are also open for evening meals. For travel directions, see under the corresponding museum or attraction.

Café Antin Kaffeliiteri £ ❶ In a little shed building next to the Antti farmstead, the café bakes traditional Finnish pastries and hard-to-find old-fashioned regional treats, including Karelian rice pastries and pancakes from the Åland Islands. ✉ Seurasaari ☎ 09 4050 9660 🕒 11.00–17.00 daily (June–Aug); 09.00–15.00 Mon–Fri, 11.00–17.00 Sat & Sun (late May & early Sept)

Café Vanille £ ❷ Opposite the church in the Russian merchants' quarter, cosy modern Café Vanille serves soups and sandwiches, along with freshly baked pastries, cappuccino, tea, hot cocoa and beer. ✉ Building C 18, Suomenlinna ☎ 040 556 1169 🌐 www.cafevanille.fi 🕒 11.00–17.00 daily (June & mid-Aug–Sept); 11.00–18.00 daily (July–mid-Aug) ❶ Open weekends only in winter

Seurasaari Island £ ❸ Several historic kiosks serve food and offer tables for those with picnics. The kiosk by the bridge (🕒 11.00–16.00 daily (June–Aug)) used to be in central Helsinki, and the kiosk in the Festival Grounds (🕒 11.00–16.00 Sat & Sun, closed Mon–Fri) has a grill available where you can barbecue your own food. ☎ 09 4050 9660

Café Bar Valimo ££ ❹ The grass-roofed ammunition foundry that houses this summer café is located on the docks near an old wooden sailing vessel and the guest harbour. Valimo serves soups, pasta dishes, snacks, sandwiches and soft drinks, as well as having a full alcohol licence. ⓐ Building B 13, Suomenlinna ⓣ 09 692 6450 ⓦ www.valimo.org ⓛ 10.00–22.00 daily (late June–late Aug); 11.00–21.00 Mon–Thur, 11.00–22.00 Fri & Sat, 11.00–17.00 Sun (May–midsummer & late Aug–mid-Sept)

Café Piper ££ ❺ In a charming old wooden villa set in a park, with a terrace overlooking the sea, Café Piper serves soups, savoury snacks, pastries and drinks including beer. ⓐ Building B 56, Suomenlinna ⓣ 09 684 1850 ⓛ 10.00–17.00 daily (May & mid-Aug–mid-Sept); 10.00–19.00 daily (June–mid-Aug)

Café Ursula ££ ❻ Café Ursula sits on the shoreline below Kaivopuisto Park. Its terrace under a sail-like canopy boasts a great view of Suomenlinna and a constant flow of shipping. It's an unbeatable location; fortunately the coffee, cakes and meals live up to it. ⓐ Ehrenströmintie 3 ⓣ 09 652 817 ⓦ http://ursula.fi/kaivopuisto ⓛ 09.00–24.00 daily

Hvitträsk ££ ❼ Located in the estate's Little Villa, the Hvitträsk café offers sandwiches and pastries, coffee, tea and alcoholic drinks in a charming atmosphere. On the second floor of the villa, the upmarket restaurant has a terrace for summer dining. An à la carte menu is offered in the evening. ⓐ Hvitträskintie 166, Luoma ⓣ 09 297 6033 ⓦ www.ravintolahvittrask.fi ⓛ Café: 11.00–18.00 daily; restaurant: 11.30–19.00 Wed–Sun, closed Mon & Tues

Korkeasaari Zoo ££ ❽ A variety of kiosks and cafés serve snacks and lunches in the summer, including Café Karhu by the Bear Castle and

Café Safari near the Mustikkamaa entrance. For a hot meal, visit Pukki Restaurant. All eateries are open during zoo opening times (see page 110). ❶ Pukki Restaurant: 09 6962 3731

Pizzeria Nikolai ££ ❾ Inside the stone casemates of Suomenlinna Fortress at King's Gate, Nikolai serves good pizza. In the summer, you can enjoy it on the terrace with a sea view. It's a good spot for a break while exploring Suomenlinna's many attractions. ⓐ Building A 10, Suomenlinna ❶ 09 668 552 ❸ 12.00–20.00 Mon–Sat, 12.00–18.00 Sun (May–Sept)

Restaurant Café Chapman ££ ❿ Near the Visitor Centre, this café with a courtyard terrace is a year-round lunch spot and on summer evenings an à la carte restaurant. ⓐ Building B 1, Suomenlinna ❶ 010 841 9195 ❸ 10.30–21.00 Mon–Fri, 12.00–21.00 Sat, 12.00–18.00 Sun (mid-May–mid-Sept); 10.30–15.00 Mon–Fri, closed Sat & Sun (mid Sept–mid-May)

Tarvaspää ££ ⓫ The villa was Gallen-Kallela's summer house until 1913 when the studio was completed. The cafeteria is now there, serving traditional freshly baked Finnish pastries, including *korvapuusti* (cinnamon buns). ⓐ Gallen-Kallelantie 27, Espoo ❶ 09 849 2340 ⓦ www.tarvaspaa.fi ❸ 11.00–18.00 daily (mid-May–Aug); 11.00–16.00 Tues–Sat, 11.00–17.00 Sun, closed Mon (Sept–mid-May)

Toy Museum Café ££ ⓬ Tucked into the wooden Russian villa with the Toy Museum, this cosy tearoom and terrace serves Russian-style tea, real lemonade and freshly baked pastries, including wonderful apple pie. ⓐ Building C 66, Suomenlinna ❶ 040 500 6607 ❸ 11.00–16.00 Sat & Sun, closed Mon–Fri (Apr–mid-May);

11.00–16.00 daily (late May); 11.00–17.00 daily (June & Aug);
11.00–18.00 daily (July); 11.00–17.00 Sat & Sun, closed Mon–Fri (Sept)

AFTER DARK

Apart from Suomenlinna, most of the 'museum islands' are daytime
destinations only. One or two restaurants might offer evening meals,
but the city's nightlife is centred in its mainland neighbourhoods.
That said, if you plan to be at one of the outlying museums, such as
Hvitträsk, in the late afternoon, the restaurants are well worth
considering for their charm and their unhurried ambience.

RESTAURANTS

Suomenlinna Klubi 20 Petty Officers' Club £–££ ⑬ Not fancy, but a
favourite place for locals to meet, the club is in one of the old wooden
buildings near the ferry landing. The terrace overlooks the city,
across the water. ⓐ Building C 8, Suomenlinna ① 09 668 273
ⓦ www.slpy.fi ⓛ 11.00–22.45 Mon–Thur, 11.00–23.45 Fri, 12.00–23.45
Sat, 12.00–19.45 Sun ① Closed mid- to late Dec

Suomenlinna Panimo Brewery Restaurant ££ ⑭ The brewery,
brewpub and restaurant are inside the high-vaulted casements of the
Jetty Barracks, built during the Russian control of the fort. Sample the
brewery's own Höpken Pils, Coyet Ale and the dark Helsinki Portteri.
Booking is recommended in the summer. ⓐ Building C 1, Suomenlinna
① 09 228 5030 ⓛ 12.00–22.00 Mon–Sat, 12.00–18.00 Sun

Helsinki by Sea Dinner Cruise ££–£££ ⑮ Enjoy a changing land and
seascape over dinner on board a sightseeing boat with a full kitchen.
The à la carte menu offers starters such as forest mushroom cream

soup or smoked salmon, and main courses including grilled breast of chicken in a Gorgonzola sauce. Book in advance for these popular evening excursions. **IHA Lines** ⓐ Meritullintori 6 ❶ 09 6874 5050 ⓦ www.ihalines.fi ❶ 19.00 Tues–Sat, closed Sun & Mon (May–Sept)

Restaurant Särkänlinna £££ ⑯ On the island of Särkkä between Suomenlinna and the southern tip of the city, the summer restaurant in a stone fortress offers stunning sea views and a setting rich in history. If you think the floor of the long dining room tilts a bit, you're right; it was designed to make it easier to get cannonballs to the cannons at the far end. ⓐ Särkkä ❶ 09 1345 6756 ⓦ www.palacekamp.fi ❶ 17.00–24.00 Mon–Sat, closed Sun (May–Sept) ❷ Reached by ferry from the Ullanlinna quay on the mainland at the southern end of the city

Walhalla Restaurant £££ ⑰ King's Gate is at the far end of the small island of Kustaanmiekka, part of the Suomenlinna island cluster, and Walhalla is set in the stone-arched interior of the fortress there. It's worth the ferry ride – an enjoyable evening trip – to savour such starters as mousse of smoked Arctic char with whitebait roe, and main courses such as fillet of reindeer with morel sauce. You can end a meal with equally traditional local ingredients: try cloudberry charlotte with cloudberry melba. The views from the terrace bar are just as outstanding as the food. Be sure to book ahead. ⓐ Building A 10, Suomenlinna ❶ 09 668 552 ⓦ www. restaurantwalhalla.com ❶ 18.00–24.00 Mon–Sat, closed Sun

❶ *The forbidding keep of Finland's largest castle is one of the sights of Turku*

OUT OF TOWN
trips

Porvoo

Porvoo lies 50 km (30 miles) northeast of Helsinki and is Finland's second-oldest town, dating from the 1500s. Today the town is known for its small shops specialising in crafts and antiques and is a perfect day-trip destination. The best way to reach Porvoo is by boat, as you can see the beautiful archipelago on the way there. **J L Runeberg** (❶ 019 524 3331 Ⓦ www.msjlruneberg.fi) and **Royal Line** (❶ 020 711 8333 Ⓦ www.royalline.fi) both offer trips to Porvoo during the summer months. Departing from Kauppatori (Market Square) in the morning, the cruise travels through the archipelago while guests enjoy lunch on board. Upon reaching the colourful old town, there are about two hours for exploring its cathedral, wooden buildings and narrow lanes lined with shops and cafés, before the return voyage to Helsinki. **Porvoo Tourist Office** ⓐ Rihkamakatu 4 ❶ 040 489 9801 Ⓦ www. porvoo.fi ❶ 09.00–18.00 Mon–Fri, 10.00–16.00 Sat & Sun (June– Aug); 09.00–16.30 Mon–Fri, 10.00–14.00 Sat, closed Sun (Sept–May)

GETTING THERE

Porvoo is only about a 30-minute drive from Helsinki. If you don't want to take a boat cruise (see above), you can either drive there on Highway E18 or take a bus. Buses to Porvoo leave every 20–30 minutes from bays 1–4 of Kamppi bus station and one-way tickets cost around €12. For timetables, consult Ⓦ www.matkahuolto.fi

SIGHTS & ATTRACTIONS

Porvoo's picturesque riverfront is lined with little red wooden buildings that were once storehouses for the city's mercantile

◯ *Porvoo's many boutiques make it a popular day-trip destination*

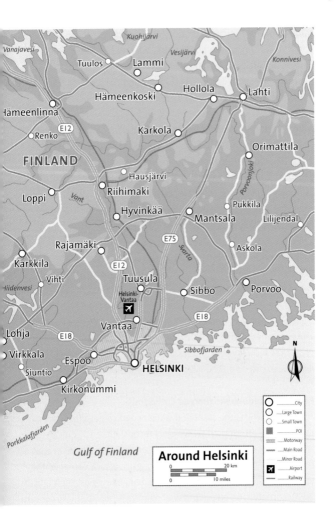

Around Helsinki

0 — 20 km
0 — 10 miles

City
Large Town
Small Town
POI
Motorway
Main Road
Minor Road
Airport
Railway

trade. The land rises from these to the old town, a charming tangle of old streets lined with ochre-coloured wooden houses in typically Finnish architecture. Two museums face the market square of the old town, one with historical collections and the other an art museum featuring the work of several *Jugendstil*-era artists.

Albert Edelfeltin ateljeemuseo (Albert Edelfelt Studio Museum)

This is where the great man painted many of his most important works. Examples from his various periods are hung liberally all over the museum, which is a must for art-lovers. ⓐ Edelfeltinpolku 3 (around 5 km (3 miles) from the town centre) ⓣ 019 577 414 ⓛ 10.00–16.00 Tues–Sun, closed Mon (June–Aug); 10.00–14.00 Tues–Sun, closed Mon (May & Sept) ⓘ Admission charge

J L Runebergin koti (House of J L Runeberg)

Even before Sparr and Edelfelt made Porvoo into an art colony, it had been a centre of creative talent. Finland's national poet, Johan Ludvig Runeberg, lived and wrote here for more than two decades from 1852 onwards, drawing other talent of his times to Porvoo. The home has been a museum since 1882. ⓐ Aleksanterinkatu 3 ⓣ 019 581 330 ⓦ www.runeberg.net ⓛ 10.00–16.00 daily (May–Sept); 10.00–16.00 Wed–Sun, closed Mon & Tues (Oct–Apr)

Porvoon tuomiokirkko (Porvoo Cathedral)

Topping the hill is the cathedral, parts of which date from the 14th century, although it was largely reconstructed a century later and became a cathedral in 1723. Further reconstruction work had to be undertaken in 2006 after an arson attack damaged the roof, but the cathedral is now fully fixed and reopened. Highlights are the ornate 1764 pulpit and wall paintings from the 15th century.

ⓐ Kirkkotori 1 ☎ 019 661 11 🕐 10.00–18.00 Mon–Fri, 10.00–14.00 Sat, 14.00–17.00 Sun (May–Sept); 10.00–14.00 Tues–Sat, 14.00–16.00 Sun, closed Mon (Oct–Apr)

TAKING A BREAK

The following represent just a small selection from the wide choice of cafés and restaurants in Porvoo.

Café Fanny £ Friendly café in an 18th-century building on the Town Hall Square in old Porvoo, serving good coffee and freshly baked cinnamon buns. ⓐ Välikatu 13 ☎ 019 582 855 🕐 09.00–17.00 daily (Apr–Aug); 10.00–16.00 Tues–Sun, closed Mon (Sept–Mar)

Porvoon Paahtimo ££ This red-tiled converted warehouse in the old historic centre of Porvoo is easy to spot. Excellent coffee choice and a river-facing terrace. ⓐ Mannerheiminkatu 2 ☎ 019 617 040 ⓦ www.porvoopaahtimo.fi 🕐 10.00–24.00 Sun–Thur, 10.00–03.00 Fri & Sat

Ravintola Wanha Laamanni £££ A top-notch restaurant in a lovely 18th-century wooden house next to the cathedral. ⓐ Vuorikatu 17 ☎ 020 752 8355 ⓦ www.wanhalaamanni.com 🕐 10.30–22.00 Mon–Fri, 12.00–22.00 Sat & Sun

ACCOMMODATION

Hotel Seurahovi ££ Centrally located, the modern building offers nicely appointed rooms, saunas, a sports bar and a restaurant. Close by, the 19th-century steam ship *Glückauf* is another good dining choice. ⓐ Rauhankatu 27 ☎ 019 547 611 ⓦ www.seurahovi.fi

Turku

Finland's oldest city at almost 800 years old, Turku was the capital until 1812. It retains key features of its medieval layout, with a castle, marketplace, cathedral and a river harbour. In Turku you will see architecture ranging from the 1200s to *Jugendstil* and the stunning modern Sibelius Museum by Woldemar Baeckman. Charming, if quiet, Turku proclaims itself as Finland's Christmas City. Visit then, or during the midsummer Medieval Festival, when the Old Great Square regains its medieval air, with craft stalls and food vendors.

Turku Touring Stop here for tourist information and maps of the southwest coast. ⓐ Aurakatu 4 ⓣ 02 262 7444 ⓦ www.turkutouring.fi ⓛ 08.30–18.00 Mon–Fri, 09.00–16.00 Sat & Sun (Apr–Sept); 10.00–15.00 Sat & Sun, closed Mon–Fri (Oct–Mar)

GETTING THERE

The easiest way to get to Turku is to take the hourly InterCity train from Helsinki Railway Station (a journey of about two hours). Train travel in Finland is reasonably priced, reliable, modern and comfortable. Although the train is the most popular method of travelling, you can also fly (ⓦ www.finnair.fi), or take a bus (ⓦ www.matkahuolto.fi).

SIGHTS & ATTRACTIONS

Apteekkimuseo ja Qwenselin talo (Pharmacy Museum & Qwensel House)

The Qwensel House, a survivor of the Great Fire, evokes the life of a well-to-do family of the early 18th century. The adjoining Pharmacy Museum shows how pharmacists prepared their own drugs.

BOAT TRIPS

Opportunities to explore the River Aura and the archipelago include everything from a free ferry to dinner-dance cruises and day sails. The City Ferry (*Föri*) crosses the Aura from early morning until midnight, year round. From June to August the Pikkuföri river ferry plies the river from the Forum Marinum (€2.50). The ***Ruissalo*** (🕿 0400 509 523 🌐 www.ruissalolautta.fi) cruises daily June–August between Turku and Ruissalo Island.

ⓐ Läntinen Rantakatu 13 🕿 02 262 0280 🌐 www.museumcentre turku.fi 🕒 10.00–18.00 Tues–Sun, closed Mon (May–mid-Sept); 10.00–16.00 Tues–Sun, closed Mon (mid-Sept–Apr) ❶ Admission charge

Forum Marinum

A combination of museum, shipyard and maritime research facility, the Forum includes two buildings (and 3,500 exhibits) and several historic vessels to tour. These include the full-rigger *Suomen Joutsen* and the minelayer *Keihässalmi*. Further upriver is the barque *Sigyn*, the world's only remaining vessel of its type. Exhibits feature navy and commercial ships, local coastal boats and culture. ⓐ Linnankatu 72 🕿 02 887 9511 🌐 www.forum-marinum.fi 🕒 11.00–19.00 daily (May–Sept); 10.00–18.00 Tues–Sun, closd Mon (Oct–Apr); ships: 11.00–19.00 daily (June–Aug) Ⓝ Bus: 1 ❶ Admission charge

Muumimaailma (Moomin World)

Finland's most famous cartoon characters, the Moomins, will please even children who did not grow up with their adventures. Moomins cavort in the story settings, such as Moominhouse, Moominpapa's Boat,

Hemulens House and the Witch's Labyrinth. At the Pancake Factory children make their own pancake and choose favourite toppings. ⓐ Naantali ⓣ 02 511 1111 ⓦ www.muumimaailma.fi ⓛ 10.00–18.00 daily (mid-June–late Aug) Ⓝ Bus: 11, 110; special bus from Turku harbour ⓘ Admission charge.

Turun linna (Turku Castle)

Built between 1280 and 1650, Finland's largest castle is a defensive pile with outer walls 3 m (10 ft) thick. Enter its maze of stairways and passages through a picturesque courtyard to find towers, banqueting halls and a chapel with medieval woodcarving. ⓐ Linnankatu 80 ⓣ 02 262 0300 ⓦ www.turunlinna.fi ⓛ 10.00–18.00 Tues–Sun, closed Mon (May–Sept); 10.00–18.00 Tues, Thur & Sun, 12.00–20.00 Wed, closed Mon & Sat (Oct–Apr) Ⓝ Bus: 1 ⓘ Admission charge

Turun tuomiokirkko (Turku Cathedral)

Work on the cathedral began in 1229, and it was part of the Holy See until the mid-16th century, when it became Finland's Lutheran mother church. Burnt or pillaged 30 times throughout its history, it has been rebuilt each time, and remains a landmark of Finnish architecture. Although its lines are familiar perpendicular Gothic, the interior is entirely plastered, without visible stonework. ⓐ Tuomiokirkkotori 20 ⓣ 02 261 7100 ⓦ www.turunseurakunnat.fi ⓛ 09.00–19.00 daily (until 20.00 summer)

Vanha Suurtori (Old Great Square)

The ensemble of old buildings near the river was the historic centre of power, both church and state, when Turku was the capital. Brinkkala Mansion was the residence of the Russian Governor General, and the stables in its courtyard are now artisans' studios. The entire square becomes a marketplace before Christmas and during the Medieval Market at the beginning of July. Ⓦ www.keskiaikaisetmarkkinat.fi

CULTURE

Aboa Vetus & Ars Nova

Built around an excavated city block of medieval Turku, Aboa Vetus explores not only the history of the site, but the archaeology of its discovery and preservation. The foundations have been dug 7 m (22 ft) deep to disclose glimpses of the medieval town, where artefacts, the stones themselves and exquisite models combine to tell the story. ⓐ Guided tours in English 11.30 daily (July & Aug)

Above, in the same building, Ars Nova couldn't be in sharper contrast to the medieval world below. More than 500 works by major contemporary and 20th-century artists from Finland and elsewhere trace movements and styles in modern art. ⓐ Itäinen Rantakatu 4–6 ⓣ 0207 181 640 Ⓦ www.aboavetusarsnova.fi ⓛ 11.00–19.00 daily (late Mar–mid-Sept); 11.00–19.00 Tues–Sun, closed Mon (Jan–late Mar & mid-Sept–mid-Dec) Ⓝ Bus: 13, 30, 55 ⓘ Admission charge

Luostarinmäen käsityöläismuseo (Luostarinmäki Handicrafts Museum)

An entire neighbourhood of 40 homes, the only ones saved from the fire that destroyed Turku in 1827, is preserved as a museum village, showing how ordinary people lived. Homes and workshops open on to little courtyards, surrounded by stables and small rooms built as families grew. About 30 artisans demonstrate period crafts, from wire weaving and printing to carving shaved-wood ornaments, and you can buy from them or from the shop (see page 136). ⓐ Luostarinmäki ⓣ 02 262 0350 ⓛ 10.00–18.00 Tues–Sun, closed Mon

 *The atrium of the Sibelius Museum doubles as a concert hall*

(May–mid-Sept), 10.00–16.00 Tues–Sun, closed Mon (mid-Sept–Apr)
Ⓝ Bus: 3, 12,18, 30 ❶ Admission charge

Sibelius-museo (Sibelius Museum)

See this for the building, even if Sibelius and music leave you cold.
Built in 1968, it was Finland's first glass and concrete building, with
concrete that simulates rough-cut wood, its organic sand colour
enhanced by lighting. Museum exhibits include rare musical
instruments, sheet music and memorabilia, with signage in English.
The atrium is a beautiful setting for Wednesday evening concerts.
ⓐ Piispankatu 17 ❶ 02 215 4494 Ⓦ www.sibeliusmuseum.abo.fi
Ⓛ 11.00–16.00 Tues–Sun, also 18.00–20.00 Wed, closed Mon
Ⓝ Bus: 4, 28, 30, 50, 51, 53, 54 ❶ Admission charge

Turun Taidemuseo (Turku Art Museum)

Prominently positioned on a hill overlooking Kauppatori, the
museum building (opened 1904) is a treasure in itself as well as
housing a fine collection of Finnish and Scandinavian art, and

playing host to diverse temporary exhibitions. ⓐ Aurakatu 26
ⓣ 02 262 7100 ⓦ www.turuntaidemuseo.fi ⓛ 11.00–19.00 Tues–Fri,
11.00–17.00 Sat & Sun, closed Mon ⓘ Admission charge (free entry
Fri evenings)

RETAIL THERAPY

Kiosks in the central square sell fresh produce, sizzling sausages,
flowers and crafts, changing with the seasons, from early morning
until 18.00 Monday to Friday and until 15.00 on Saturday.
Overlooking this is the large **Sokos** department store (ⓐ Eerikinkatu 11
ⓣ 010 765 020) and from the square's upper corner runs
Kauppiaskatu, the main shopping street. Small shops are scattered
through the central streets around the market square and two
shopping centres – Hansa and Forum – are close by.

Antiikkiliike Wanha Elias Shop or browse for antique furniture and
decorative pieces. ⓐ Eerikinkatu 29 ⓣ 0400 846 817 ⓦ www.
antiikkiliikewanhaelias.fi ⓛ 10.00–17.00 Mon–Fri, 10.00–13.00 Sat,
closed Sun

Au-Holmberg Oy This provides a fascinating insight into the
goldsmith's craft. ⓐ Itäinen Rantakatu 64 ⓣ 02 231 6419 ⓦ www.au-
holmberg.fi ⓛ 10.00–16.30 Mon–Fri, closed Sat & Sun

Fatabur The museum shop at Turku Castle sells a well-chosen
selection of tasteful gifts, including historic glassware and jewellery
reproductions, as well as traditional crafts (see page 132 for contact
details). ⓛ 10.00–17.45 Tues–Sun, closed Mon (May–Sept);
10.00–17.45 Tues, Thur & Sun, 12.00–19.45 Wed (Oct–Apr)

Föripuoti Traditional and contemporary Finnish crafts.
ⓐ Sairashuoneenkatu 1 ⓣ 02 233 1073 ⓛ 10.00–14.00 Mon–Wed &
Fri, 10.00–17.30 Thur, closed Sat & Sun

Iittala Outlet Finnish design, from glassware and china to cooking
pots, in a factory outlet store. ⓐ Hämeenkatu 6 ⓣ 020 439 3547
ⓛ 10.00–20.00 Mon–Fri, 10.00–18.00 Sat, closed Sun

Piha-Puoti (Luostarinmäki Handicrafts Museum Shop) The products
of these authentic workshops are sold in the museum's shop (see
page 133 for contact details). ⓛ 10.00–17.45 Tues–Sun, closed Mon
(May–Sept & Dec–early Jan)

Skanssi Turku's newest shopping mall is architecturally striking –
and there's an adventure park, **Flowpark** (ⓣ 0400 864 862 ⓦ www.
flowpark.fi ⓛ 12.00–20.00 Mon–Sat, closed Sun (Jun–mid-Aug);
shorter hours Wed–Sun, closed Mon & Tues (May–Oct) ⓘ Admission
charge), right in the middle of the complex. ⓐ Skanssinkatu 10 B
ⓣ 040 195 3742 ⓦ www.skanssi.fi ⓛ 08.00–21.00 Mon–Fri, 08.00–
18.00 Sat, 12.00–18.00 Sun ⓘ Bus: 9 from Kauppatori

Turku Market Hall In a traditional indoor market atmosphere, 50
merchants offer speciality foods, produce and crafts. ⓐ Eerikinkatu 16
ⓛ 07.00–17.30 Mon–Fri, 07.00–15.00 Sat, closed Sun

TAKING A BREAK

Stop at the market square for sausages or other quick foods. ou'll
also find food stalls in the market hall and at the two big open-air
markets that fill Old Great Square in December and July.

Café Qwensel £ A delightful courtyard behind the Qwensel House is home to this summer café serving the best cherry pie in Turku. ⓐ Läntinen Rantakatu 13 ❶ 02 262 0280 ⑤ 10.00–18.00 Tues–Sun, closed Mon (May–mid-Sept); 10.00–16.00 Tues–Sun, closed Mon (mid-Sept–Apr)

Puutorin Vessa £ Sometimes it helps if you don't speak Finnish, especially when a pub's name translates to 'The Wood Market's Toilet'. This one is in a much-converted WC, hence the name – another example of the Finns' wicked sense of humour. Snack food is available along with a good selection of beers. ⓐ Puutori ❶ 02 233 8123 ⓦ www.puutorinvessa.fi ⑤ 12.00–24.00 daily

Koulu £–££ Housed in a restored school (*koulu* means 'school'), this brewery serves house beers and others, along with lunch and dinner. ⓐ Eerikinkatu 18 ❶ 02 274 5757 ⓦ www.panimoravintola koulu.fi ⑤ 11.00–02.00 Sun–Thur, 11.00–03.00 Fri & Sat. Food served 11.00–24.00 Mon–Fri, 12.00–24.00 Sat

Café Restaurant Daphne ££ Stay in the maritime spirit at the Forum Marinum (see page 131) with a light lunch or more substantial evening meal at this cheery café-restaurant, which boasts a full-size sailing boat inside. ⓐ Linnankatu 72 ❶ 02 337 3800 ⓦ www.forum-marinum.fi ⑤ 11.00–17.00 Mon–Fri, 12.00–17.00 Sat & Sun

Café Restaurant Aula ££ For a break from the very different worlds of medieval life and 21st-century art, stop for coffee at this tidy little café. ⓐ Aboa Vetus & Ars Nova, Itäinen Rantakatu 4–6 ❶ 020 718 1649 ⑤ 11.00–18.00 daily (Apr–Sept); 11.00–18.00 Tues–Sun, closed Mon (Oct–Mar)

Cafeteria Domcafé ££ Tucked into the brick vaults below the cathedral, this café serves excellent coffee and cakes from traditional recipes. ⓐ Entrance at the cathedral steps ⓣ 02 261 7310 ⓛ Daily in summer & first three weekends in December

AFTER DARK

Along with several outstanding restaurants well worth spending an evening in, Turku has a rich cultural scene, with theatres, two orchestras, jazz and rock bars. The Turku Music Festival and Rockfestival Ruisrock are among the oldest in the Nordic countries.

RESTAURANTS

Pavilion Vaakahuone £–££ Go for the fish, go for the swing and Dixieland, or go for the summer scene at the river. Choose from several menus all grouped around the same terrace – seafood, pizza, giant Bratwurst and a coffee shop. Live music every night. ⓐ Linnankatu 38 ⓣ 02 515 3300 ⓦ www.vaakahuone.fi ⓛ Daylight hours May–Aug (which means most of the night)

Pub Old Bank £–££ Everyone meets at this popular pub in a historic *Jugendstil* bank building, where they serve 150 different beers in an English-style bar atmosphere. The food is good, too. ⓐ Aurakatu 3 ⓦ www.oldbank.fi ⓣ 02 274 5700 ⓛ 12.00–24.00 Mon & Sun, 12.00–02.00 Tues–Thur, 12.00–03.00 Fri & Sat

Cindyn Salonki ££ Uncomplicated dishes, many based on local seafood, are served in a boat moored on the river. ⓐ Itäinen Rantakatu ⓣ 02 250 2300 ⓦ www.cindy.fi ⓛ 11.00–23.00 Mon–Fri, 12.00–24.00 Sat, 13.00–21.00 Sun

Foija ££ Beneath the sleek modern Hansa shopping centre beside Kauppatori, you're in for a surprise as you find yourself in a brick-vaulted cellar dating back to 1839. History is paid homage with 19th-, 20th- and 21st-century menus. ❸ Aurakatu 10 (entrance through Hemingway's bar) ☎ 02 251 8665 ⓦ www.foija.fi ⏰ 11.00–22.00 Mon & Tues, 11.00–23.00 Wed & Thur, 11.00–24.00 Fri, 12.00–24.00 Sat, 12.00–20.00 Sun

Enkeliravintola ££–£££ The name of this restaurant translates as 'angel restaurant' and the food is indeed heavenly. Begin with a cup of warming *glögi*, while you look around at the playful décor. Then order dishes based on creative interpretations of Finnish cuisine: game terrine with lingonberries, *pot-au-feu* of lightly smoked pork or vegetarian mushroom pie. ❸ Kauppiaskatu 16 ☎ 02 231 8088 ⓦ www.enkeliravintola.fi ⏰ 11.00–15.00 Mon, 11.00–22.00 Tues–Fri, 13.00–22.00 Sat, 13.00–20.00 Sun

Herman ££–£££ An upmarket brewery-cum-restaurant in an attractive former warehouse on the waterfront, midway between the castle and the cathedral. Lunch buffets are excellent value, the evening à la carte more pricey. ❸ Läntinen Rantakatu 37 ☎ 02 230 3333 ⓦ www.ravintolaherman.com ⏰ 11.00–14.00, 17.00–22.00 Tues–Fri, 15.00–22.00 Sat, closed Sun & Mon

Pinella ££–£££ This historic eatery (it claims to be Finland's oldest) near the cathedral reopened in 2011 following extensive renovation. Enjoy classic cuisine under the colonnade or sample delicious cakes on the summer terrace overlooking the river. ❸ Vanha Suurtori 2 ☎ 02 445 6500 ⓦ www.pinella.fi ⏰ 11.00–23.00 Mon–Fri, 12.00–23.00 Sat, 12.00–20.00 Sun

BARS & CLUBS

Galax A sleek dance club and late-night restaurant, which hosts well-known Finnish performers. Minimum age is 24 at weekends. ⓐ Aurakatu 6 ⓣ 02 284 3300 ⓞ 21.00–02.00 Wed, 21.00–04.00 Thur–Sat, closed Sun–Tues

ACCOMMODATION

Best Western Hotel Seaport ££ Located in a charming converted customs warehouse in the dock area, this makes a good choice if you are cruising in or out of Turku on a Baltic ferry. ⓐ Matkustajasatama ⓣ 02 283 3000 ⓦ www.bestwestern.com

Park Hotel ££ This family-run hotel in a quiet neighbourhood is handy for the railway station and close to Kauppatori, too. Soft beds, individually decorated rooms – all in all, a world away from corporate blandness. ⓐ Rauhankatu 1 ⓣ 02 273 2555 ⓦ www.parkhotelturku.fi

Naantali Spa ££–£££ Saunas and aromatic aquatherapy are only the beginning of the facilities offered at this state-of-the-art resort spa near Turku. From the huge indoor pool, dive under the glass wall and stare at the winter sky from a steaming outdoor pool. ⓐ Naantali ⓣ 02 445 5100 ⓦ www.naantalispa.fi

Ruissalo Spa Hotel ££–£££ Pamper youself at this elegant spa on Ruissalo Island. A large, modern resort, its rooms are smart and there are several restaurants. The sport and spa facilities are superb. ⓐ Ruissalon puistotie 640 ⓣ 02 445 5100 ⓦ www.ruissalospa.fi

● *Helsinki Railway Station boasts Eliel Saarinen's most famous interior*

PRACTICAL
information

Directory

GETTING THERE

Helsinki can be reached by direct daily flights from many major
European hubs. Its location on the Baltic makes ferries a popular
method of transport from Stockholm and from ports in Estonia and
Germany. Most of these ferries also carry cars, so Finland can be
incorporated into a driving holiday.

By air

Finnair flies to Helsinki-Vantaa (see page 50) from many UK and
European airports, including several flights daily from Heathrow and

⬥ *Helsinki-Vantaa Airport is Finland's largest modern gateway*

Manchester. British Airways also has direct flights from Heathrow, while easyJet flies to Vantaa from Gatwick and Manchester. Blue1 flies to Helsinki from Heathrow and also, in the summer, from Edinburgh.

Finnair operates daily direct flights from JFK in New York and, in the summer, from Toronto. SAS flies from New York, Washington and Chicago, but always connecting through Stockholm or Copenhagen.

Blue1 Ⓦ www.blue1.com
British Airways Ⓦ www.britishairways.com
easyJet Ⓦ www.easyjet.com
Finnair Ⓦ www.finnair.com
SAS Ⓦ www.flysas.com

Many people are aware that air travel emits CO_2, which contributes to climate change. You may be interested in the possibility of lessening the environmental impact of your flight through the charity **Climate Care** (Ⓦ www.climatecare.org), which offsets your CO_2 by funding environmental projects around the world.

By rail

Train travel is possible as far as Stockholm, from which point you must take a ferry. The trip from London's St Pancras International to Stockholm takes just over 18 hours, by Eurostar to Brussels, with changes in Cologne and Copenhagen. The monthly *Thomas Cook European Rail Timetable* has up-to-date schedules for European international and national train services. Travellers from outside Europe who plan to use trains should investigate the various multi-day and multi-country train passes offered by Rail Europe. Eurail Selectpass includes rail travel in all four Nordic countries (or any combination of them) plus Germany, with even greater savings for two or more people travelling together.

Eurostar 🕐 (UK) 08432 186 186 Ⓦ www.eurostar.com
Rail Europe Ⓦ www.raileurope.co.uk
Thomas Cook European Rail Timetable 🕐 (UK) 01733 416477;
(USA) 1 800 322 3834 Ⓦ www.thomascookpublishing.com

By road

Rock-bottom airfares apart, the cheapest way to Helsinki from the UK is by coach, with Eurolines from London's Victoria Coach Station to Tallinn in Estonia. From here ferries, including high-speed catamarans, regularly make the short crossing to Finland, arriving close to Helsinki's city centre.

Eurolines 🕐 08717 818181 Ⓦ www.eurolines.com

Car trips to Finland from the UK are possible without taking a ferry (use Eurotunnel and then make a long loop through northern Sweden around the Gulf of Bothnia), but the shortest and usually cheapest route is again via Tallinn in Estonia (the Via Baltica).

Cars in Finland drive on the right-hand side of the road. For rules, speed limits and safety tips for drivers, see page 51.

By sea

Sweden, Germany and Estonia are all connected to Finland by ferry links. Tallink Silja operates a useful service from Rostock in Germany to Helsinki four days a week, with the journey taking around 26 hours. The same company has around seven departures every day to Helsinki from Tallinn, Estonia (taking two hours) and nightly departures from Stockholm, Sweden. Viking Line operates both day and night journeys between Stockholm and Helsinki, as well as two departures per day from Tallinn to Helsinki.

Tallink Silja Ⓦ www.tallinksilja.com
Viking Line Ⓦ www.vikingline.fi

ENTRY FORMALITIES

Citizens of the UK, Republic of Ireland, USA, Canada and Australia need only a valid passport to enter Finland and do not require visas. Citizens of EU countries other than the UK need only a valid national identity card, or a passport. Citizens of South Africa must have a passport and visa to enter. Visa forms can be obtained from your nearest Finnish embassy or consulate.

EU citizens can bring goods for personal use when arriving from another EU country, but quantities of tobacco and alcohol must be sensible amounts for personal use. Limits for non-EU nationals are 200 cigarettes and one litre of spirits or two litres of wine.

MONEY

The currency in Finland is the euro (€), which is divided into 100 cents. Notes are in €5, 10, 20, 50, 100, 200 and 500 denominations and coins are €1 and €2, plus 5, 10, 20 and 50 cents. 1- and 2-cent coins are not used in Finland, and prices in shops are generally rounded to the nearest 5 cents. The best means of obtaining local currency is by using a debit card. Although many banks charge a fee for this, these are usually less than cash advances on credit cards, and are at a more favourable exchange rate than cash transactions or traveller's cheques. ATMs (cashpoints) can be found nearly everywhere, easily recognised by yellow hoods. Finns call an ATM an *Otto*.

Credit cards are very widely used in Helsinki, even by taxis, and you can often pay by credit card in pubs and get cash back if you're short. Traveller's cheques can be cashed at banks, post offices and in most hotels, and are widely accepted in major shops and stores in Helsinki.

Bureaux de change can be found in airports and near the railway station. You can also change money at Helsinki's large bank **Nordea** (Main branch: ❷ Aleksanterinkatu 30 ❶ 02 007 000 ❸ 10.00–16.30 Mon–Fri, closed Sat & Sun).

HEALTH, SAFETY & CRIME

Finnish medical care is excellent, with English-speaking doctors and modern clinics and hospitals. Free emergency services are available to all visitors. Citizens from the European Union (and

❍ *Gigantic* Jugendstil *guardians of Helsinki Railway Station*

a few other European countries) can also claim free treatment
for more minor complaints on production of a European
Health Insurance Card (EHIC). All visitors, but particularly
those without an EHIC, should make sure that they take out
adequate travel insurance.

If you are there in the winter and take part in winter sports,
remember that the thickness of ice on lakes and bays is hard to judge.
Skate or walk on ice only with a trained guide or where a number of
others are also on the ice. Never venture on to ice alone, even if you
think you are sure of its strength.

Finland is one of the safest countries in the world in which to travel, but remember that wherever tourists gather, there will be occasional pickpockets. Lock valuables in the hotel safe or leave them at home. You are not likely to need your diamond tiara in Helsinki.

OPENING HOURS

Most shops are open from 09.00 to between 16.00 and 18.00 on Monday to Friday, and from 09.00 to between 14.00 and 16.00 on Saturday. Shops are not open on Sunday except in the summer and the run-up to Christmas.

TOILETS

Public facilities are common in Helsinki, but they may not be open all hours. Those inside buildings such as the public markets close with the market. Toilets in parks may be open limited hours and closed on Sundays and in the winter. Those in hotels and cafés are a good alternative when others are closed.

CHILDREN

Finns are fond of children and frequently take their own out and about, so most hotels and restaurants are prepared. Those with music and entertainment, as well as other nightspots, do not welcome children any more than their equivalents would in any city. However, Helsinki has plenty of family-friendly attractions.

Korkeasaari Zoo (see page 109) is worthwhile for the entire family, with rare cats (including snow leopards), red pandas, a specialist collection of animals indigenous to the Arctic and, by contrast, many Amazonian species in the Amazonia microclimate house. The trip there by ferry is fun for children, too.

For the underwater 'zoo' experience, you can take them to **Sea Life Helsinki** (see page 90), which explores marine life while offering aquatic adventures. Nearby is Linnanmäki Amusement Park (see page 88), the perfect place to keep kids amused all day with rides, a monorail, an open-air theatre, eating places that welcome children and a free playground. And to make you feel good about every euro you spend on rides, all the income goes to the national child welfare organisations that run the park.

It's almost guaranteed that you'll enjoy playing at the **Helsinki Playground** (see page 66) just as much as the children do. Plenty of access to all the hands-on activities is assured by timed ticketing. Choose your two-hour time slot, at 10.00, 12.00, 14.00, 16.00 or 18.00.

The **Serena Waterpark** (ⓐ Torniaentie 10, Espoo ⓣ 09 887 0550 ⓦ www.serena.fi ⓛ 11.00–20.00 daily ⓝ Bus: 339. ⓘ Admission charge) is a bit out of town, but reachable by bus from the central bus station in Helsinki. This is a good diversion if the weather turns hot in the summer, or when you need a breath of the tropics on a wintry day. Children won't believe that a water park stays open in the winter. It's a low-key splash park, but good for young children. If you're in Turku, there's the **Flowpark** adventure park at the Skanssi shopping centre (see page 136) as well as the huge new **JukuPark** water park, 3 km (1.6 miles) from the city centre, boasting 16 flumes and a host of other attractions. ⓣ 02 262 7444 ⓦ www.jukupark.fi ⓛ 11.00–19.00 Mon–Fri, 11.00–19.00 Sat & Sun (early–late June); 11.00–19.00 daily (late June–mid-Aug) ⓝ Bus: 13, 28

Performances for children are staged on Suomenlinna Island during the summer, with a variety of shows and theatre companies participating. The Helsinki City Tourist & Convention Bureau (see page 153) will have schedules. Older children will enjoy exploring the fortress and, as with the zoo, the boat ride there is an adventure itself. They will also enjoy the hands-on activities at Seurasaari Open-Air Museum, as well as the unusual old buildings.

COMMUNICATIONS

Internet

Public Internet access is widely available in Helsinki and other large towns, with plenty of Internet cafés and public libraries offering access. Many hotels have a computer or broadband connection available for guests, but check the Wi-Fi charges first.

A reliable Internet café in the centre is **Waynes Coffee** (ⓐ Kaisaniemenkatu 3 ⓣ 040 413 9401 ⓛ 08.00–21.00 Mon–Fri,

TELEPHONING HELSINKI

The country code for Finland is 358. The city code for Helsinki is 09, for Turku 02, for Porvoo 019. To call from outside Finland, dial the international access code of the country you're calling from (00 from the UK, 001 from the US), then 358, then the Finnish city code (omitting the first 0), and finally the local number you require. From inside Finland, dial the city code and number. Note that there is no set length for local Finnish telephone numbers.

TELEPHONING ABROAD

To make an international call from Finland, dial 00, then the country code (UK 44, Republic of Ireland 353, USA and Canada 1, Australia 61, New Zealand 64, South Africa 27) and the area code (omitting the initial zero in UK area codes) and then the number you require.

10.00–21.00 Sat, 12.00–21.00 Sun). If you want to read your emails and have a good night out at the same time, try **Mbar** (ⓐ Lasipalatsi/Mannerheimintie 22–24 ⓣ 09 6124 5420 ⓦ www. mbar.fi ⓛ 09.00–24.00 Mon & Tues, 09.00–02.00 Wed & Thur, 09.00–03.00 Fri & Sat, 12.00–24.00 Sun), which offers computers and a WLAN connection for customers as well as DJs every night.

Phone

Due in part to extremely high levels of mobile phone usage in Finland, public telephones are not used. Your best option is to buy a pre-paid Finnish SIM card for your own mobile. Before making a call from your hotel room, check the rates: they can often be extortionate.

Post

Finnish post is not only prompt, it is safe; the Finns are honest to their toes, so what you mail will arrive safely and quickly. Helsinki's main post office is **Posti Central Office** (ⓐ Elielinaukio 2 ⓣ 0200 71000 ⓛ 07.00–21.00 Mon–Fri, 10.00–18.00 Sat & Sun). A postcard should arrive at EU destinations within three to four days and will take around a week to reach North America.

ELECTRICITY

Current in Finland is 220V AC, at 50 Hz. Australian, New Zealand, US, Canadian, South African and UK appliances will need adaptors to fit Finnish sockets. If you are travelling in other Nordic countries, note that sockets are not all the same. Appliances using only 110V will need transformers, as well as plug adaptors.

MEDIA

Helsinki's newspaper *Helsingin Sanomat* publishes an online digest in English, good for local news and events. International newspapers are available at newsstands and in hotels. For information on current events, contact the tourist office or consult the brochures and magazines listed on page 32.

⬥ *Ferries drop their passengers right into the very heart of Helsinki*

TRAVELLERS WITH DISABILITIES

Lifts provide access to all floors (including the subterranean tunnels that connect much of the central area) in the major department stores and shopping centres, as well as the railway station and Kinopalatsi cinema centre. When using the tunnels, you can return to street level through these buildings or by a number of lifts across the system. The zoo, Suomenlinna Fortress, the Ateneum and a number of other tourist sights have disabled access to most of their facilities, as do the Opera House and Finlandia Hall. The outdoor areas of Seurasaari Open-Air Museum are accessible, but the historic buildings are not.

There is normally space in Finnish trains for wheelchairs, as well as special tables, allowing for wheelchair manoeuvres. These spaces need reservations, but there is normally no extra charge.

For specially equipped taxis, call one of the following:

Helsingin Palveluauto Oy ⓐ Helsingin Palveluauto ⓣ 020 743 2150
Invataxi Iiro's Taxi Service ⓣ 040 500 6070

TOURIST INFORMATION

Helsinki City Tourist & Convention Bureau ⓐ Pohjoisesplanadi 19, Helsinki ⓣ 09 3101 3300 ⓦ www.visithelsinki.fi ⓛ 09.00–20.00 Mon–Fri, 09.00–18.00 Sat & Sun (mid-May–mid-Sept); 09.00–18.00 Mon–Fri, 10.00–16.00 Sat & Sun (mid-Sept–mid-May)

Visitors from the UK can contact the London branch of the **Finnish Tourist Board** ⓐ PO Box 33213, London W6 8JX ⓣ 020 783 6200 ⓦ www.visitfinland.com ⓔ finlandinfolon@mek.fi

Emergencies

Police, ambulance or fire emergency number 📞 112

MEDICAL SERVICES

Should you become ill in Finland, it's good to know that most medical personnel speak good English. The consular office of your embassy can provide a list. You can also go prepared with the appropriate pages from the directory published by the **International Association of Medical Assistance for Travellers** (IAMAT).
🌐 www.iamat.org

The Haartman Hospital provides 24-hour medical and dental treatment. 📍 Haartmaninkatu 4 📞 09 310 3461

POLICE

For non-urgent police assistance, visit the **main police station** (📍 Punanotkonkatu 2 📞 071 877 0111). There is a more central precinct at 📍 Pieni Roobertinkatu 1–3 📞 071 877 4715

EMERGENCY PHRASES

Help!	**Help me, please!**
Apua!	Voitko auttaa!
Erpuer!	*Voytko owttah!*

Call an ambulance/Call a doctor/Call the police!
Soittakaaa ambulanssi/Kutsukaa lääkäri/Soittakaaa poliisi!
Soi-terkah ermbulernsi/Kutsukah lahkari/Soi-terkah polleesi!

Lost property

Police Lost Property Office ⓐ Punanotkonkatu 2 ⓣ 071 877 3180
ⓛ 08.00–16.15 Mon–Fri, closed Sat & Sun (enquiries by phone
10.00–14.00 Mon–Fri) Ⓝ Tram: 10

Transport Lost Property For items lost on trains, buses, trams and at
the airport. You can make enquiries by telephone. ⓐ Mäkelänkatu 56
ⓣ 0600 410 06 ⓦ www.loytotavara.net ⓛ 09.00–18.00 Mon–Fri,
10.00–14.00 Sat, closed Sun

EMBASSIES & CONSULATES

Consulates and consular sections of embassies handle emergencies
of travelling citizens. After reporting it to the police, your consulate
or embassy should be the first place you turn to if a passport is lost
or stolen.

Australian Consulate ⓐ Museokatu 25 B ⓣ 09 4777 6640
ⓔ australian.consulate@tradimex.fi

British Embassy ⓐ Itäinen puistotie 17 ⓣ 09 228 65100
ⓦ http://ukinfinland.fco.gov.uk ⓛ 08.30–15.30 Mon–Fri, closed Sat &
Sun (late June–late Aug); 09.00–17.00 daily (rest of year)

Canadian Embassy ⓐ Pohjoisesplanadi 25 B ⓣ 09 228 530
ⓦ www.canada.fi

Irish Embassy ⓐ Erottajankatu 7 A ⓣ 09 646 006

New Zealand Consulate ⓐ Erottajankatu 9 ⓣ 050 342 9950

South African Embassy ⓐ Rahapajankatu 1 A 5 (3rd Floor)
ⓣ 09 6860 3100 ⓦ www.southafricanembassy.fi ⓛ Consular
hours 09.00–12.30 Mon–Fri, closed Sat & Sun

United States Embassy, Consular Office ⓐ Itäinen puistotie 14 B
ⓣ 09 616 250 ⓔ finland@usembassy.gov ⓛ 09.00–12.00 Mon–Thur,
closed Fri–Sun; phone hours: 14.00–16.00 Mon–Thur

ACKNOWLEDGEMENTS

Thomas Cook wishes to thank the photographers, picture libraries and other organisations, to whom the copyright belongs, for the photographs in this book.

A1 PIX pages 108–9, 152; DREAMSTIME.COM page 5 (Ruta Saulyte-Laurinaviciene); ISTOCKPHOTO.COM page 18 (Dainis Derics); FINNISH TOURIST BOARD pages 27, 34, 46, 89, 142; TERO PUHA pages 7, 21, 39, 42–3, 61; STILLMAN ROGERS pages 8, 17, 23, 49, 69, 78, 82, 92–3, 123, 125, 134, 141, 146–7; JON SPARKS pages 11, 15, 59, 72–3, 90, 100, 116; WIKIMEDIA COMMONS page 33.

For CAMBRIDGE PUBLISHING MANAGEMENT LIMITED:
Project editor: Tom Lee
Layout: Paul Queripel
Proofreaders: Kate Taylor & Rosalind Munro

Send your thoughts to
books@thomascook.com

- Found a great bar, club, shop or must-see sight that we don't feature?
- Like to tip us off about any information that needs a little updating?
- Want to tell us what you love about this handy little guidebook and more importantly how we can make it even handier?

Then here's your chance to tell all! Send us ideas, discoveries and recommendations today and then look out for your valuable input in the next edition of this title.

Email the above address (stating the title) or write to:
pocket guides Series Editor, Thomas Cook Publishing, PO Box 227, Coningsby Road, Peterborough PE3 8SB, UK.

WHAT'S IN YOUR GUIDEBOOK?

Independent authors Impartial up-to-date information from our travel experts who meticulously source local knowledge.

Experience Thomas Cook's 165 years in the travel industry and guidebook publishing enriches every word with expertise you can trust.

Travel know-how Thomas Cook has thousands of staff working around the globe, all living and breathing travel.

Editors Travel-publishing professionals, pulling everything together to craft a perfect blend of words, pictures, maps and design.

You, the traveller We deliver a practical, no-nonsense approach to information, geared to how you really use it.

Useful phrases

English	Finnish	Approx pronunciation
BASICS		
Yes	Joo	*Yoo*
No	Ei	*Aye*
Please	Kiitos/Ole hyvä	*Keetoss/Oleh hewva*
Thank you	Kiitos	*Keetoss*
Hello	Hei	*Hey*
Goodbye	Näkemiin	*Nakehmeen*
Excuse me	Anteeksi	*Erntehksi*
Sorry	Sori	*Sorry*
That's okay	Ole hyvä	*Oleh hewva*
I don't speak Finnish	En puhu suomea	*En puhu suormeah*
Do you speak English?	Puhutko englantia?	*Puhutko ehnglerntier?*
Good morning	Hyvää huomenta	*Hewva-a huomehnter*
Good afternoon	Hyvää päivää	*Hewva-a pa-i-va-a*
Good evening	Hyvää iltaa	*Hewva-a iltah*
Goodnight	Hyvää yötä	*Hewva-a ew-erta*
My name is ...	Minun nimeni on ...	*Minun nimehni on ...*
NUMBERS		
One	Yksi	*Ewksi*
Two	Kaksi	*Kerksi*
Three	Kolme	*Kolmeh*
Four	Neljä	*Nehlyah*
Five	Viisi	*Veesi*
Six	Kuusi	*Koosi*
Seven	Seitsemän	*Sehtsehman*
Eight	Kahdeksan	*Kerdehksern*
Nine	Yhdeksän	*Ewkh-dehksan*
Ten	Kymmenen	*Kewmehnehn*
Twenty	Kaksikymmentä	*Kerksikewmehnta*
Fifty	Viisikymmentä	*Veesikewmehnta*
One hundred	Sata	*Ser-ter*
SIGNS & NOTICES		
Airport	Lentokenttä	*Lenthokenthae*
Railway station	Rautatieasema	*Rawtahtie-ah-sehmah*
Platform	Laituri	*Laytuhri*
Smoking/Non-smoking	Tupakointi/ Tupakointi kielletty	*Tupahkhointi/ Tuphakhointi kie-lettue*
Toilets	WC/Vessa	*Veesee/Vessah*
Ladies/Gentlemen	Naiset/Miehet	*Naihset/Miehet*
Metro/Tram/Bus	Metro/Raitiovaunu/Bussi	*Metro/Rayti-o-vawnu/Bussi*